Sign Gallery International

Award-winning designs from the Editors of Signs of the Times

ST Publications
Cincinnati, Ohio

ISBN: 0-944094-33-3

Published by:
ST Publications, Inc.
Book Division
407 Gilbert Avenue
Cincinnati, Ohio 45202
Tel. 513-421-2050
Fax 513-421-6110

Distributed to the book and art trade in the U.S. and Canada by:
Watson-Guptill Publications
1515 Broadway
New York, NY 10036
Tel. 908-363-4511
Fax 908-363-0338

Distributed to the rest of the world by:
Hearst Books International
1350 Avenue of the Americas
New York, NY 10003
Tel. 212-261-6770
Fax 212-261-6795

Printed in China

10 9 8 7 6 5 4 3 2 1

Introduction

Sign design has benefitted greatly from continuing technological advances in graphic design software, and the electronic, vinyl and foam materials used in fabrication. This book includes photos of signs derived from the best technology has to offer.

SIGNS OF THE TIMES

Contents

Introduction   3

Electric Signs   6

Original logo / freestanding or ground   8

Original logo / mounted or projecting   18

Existing logo / freestanding or ground   28

Existing logo / mounted or projecting   36

Sign systems   44

Digital display   56

Exposed neon   62

Neon art / sculpture   70

Neon lighting / graphics   74

Multi-tenant   80

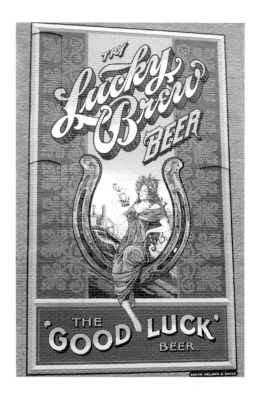

Commercial Signs — 84

Flat signs / freestanding or ground — 86

Flat signs / mounted or projecting — 94

Dimensional / freestanding or ground — 102

Dimensional / mounted or projecting — 110

Window lettering / graphics — 120

Wall murals / supergraphics — 126

Vehicle graphics — 132

Banners — 140

Glass signs — 146

Sign systems — 152

Entry monuments — 164

Temporary site signs — 170

Brazil / Special section — 178

Index of fabricators — 188

Index of designers — 190

Fabricator
Neon Knights, Inc.
Baltimore, MD
Designer
Marsha D. Lidard
Neon Knights, Inc.

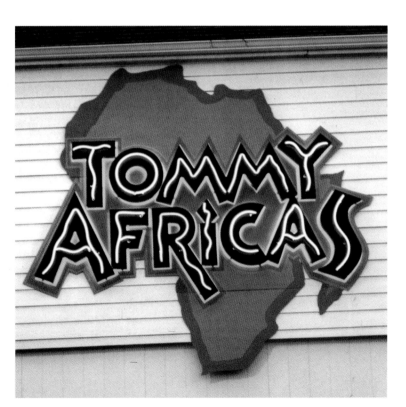

Fabricator
National Sign Corp.
Seattle, WA
Designer
Ken Krumpos
National Sign Corp.

Fabricator
Neon-Line Werbedesign GmbH.
Vienna, Austria
Designers
Dusty Sprengnagel (sign design)
Dusty Sprengnagel and Alfred Hager (tower design)
Neon-Line Werbedesign GmbH.

Fabricator
Ultraneon Sign Co.
San Diego, CA
Designer
Graphic Solutions
San Diego, CA

Fabricator
Creative Neon Works, Inc.
Dartmouth, NS
Canada
Designer
Creative Neon Works, Inc.

The customer wanted something that suggested a 50s diner. The sign incorporates a pole left over from a fluorescent sign. The steel structure is constructed of satin-coat sheetmetal with an enamel finish, vinyl graphics, chrome Mylar® polyester and exposed neon. The interior neon is ruby red and bromo blue.

Fabricator
National Sign Corp.
Seattle, WA
Designer
Ken Krumpos
National Sign Corp.
Selling price
$12,000

This double-faced, illuminated, monument display spans 8 ft. 6 in. × 10 ft. The background is aluminum painted with a gloss black, with matte green leaves and purple grapes. The double-tube neon "Grazie's" is surface-applied. An illuminated box spells out "Ristorante Italiano." The cut-out zigzag has a neon accent on top. The support is purposefully mounted off-center for this asymmetric design.

Fabricators
Simington Electrical Adv./Sign Div.
Downey, CA

Tower Structures
Chula Vista, CA
Designers
Jim Simington
Simington Electrical Adv./Sign Div.

Noel Davies & Assoc.
Beverly Hills, CA
Selling price
$187,000

This 90-ft. tower is fabricated from galvanized steel supports and light-absorbing fiberglass panels. The lower ID aluminum panels are routed and have filled-in letters. At the tower base, 21 independent spotlights are computer-driven to change multi-colors and intermittently illuminate the tower. The tower also houses Airtouch Cellular's full antenna array for all of Southern California and surrounding areas.

Fabricator
Imperial Sign Corp.
Port Coquitlam, BC
Canada
Designer
David Hornblow
The Design Works
Vancouver, BC
Canada
Account executive
Lindsay Miles
Selling price
$24,000 (Canadian)

This sign has a 7 × 8-ft. outside diameter. The aluminum display has an open-channel, ruby-neon "B" cut into a striped oval. "Beatty St." is a separate cabinet with ½-in. clear Plexiglas® acrylic, pushed-through copy. The oversized aluminum faces are painted yellow. Two 4 × 4-in.-high strength-steel supports are lagged into the brick/concrete, which makes the sign 28 ft. tall.

Fabricator
Orde Adv. Inc.
DePere, WI
Designer
Rhoda Schley-Diny
Orde Adv. Inc.
Account executive
Kelli Claflin

This 22 ft., 3-in.-tall × 32 ft., 9-in.-wide main ID sign needed to convey the woodland surroundings of this rural casino. The pine trees were constructed in sections from an angle-iron framework. The painted aluminum faces and sides include 15mm vine-green argon that illuminates the tree shapes. The channel letters and illuminated logo were built separately from the main cabinet. They utilize aluminum, Plexiglas® acrylic, neon, paint and vinyl on flexible-face material. Fluorescent lamps illuminate it. The 24 ft., 6-in.-tall base is formed concrete finished with a stone veneer that's used in the architecture of the new building. Rolled-aluminum capping finishes the top of the base.

Fabricators
Image Works, Inc.
Ashland, VA

Living Color, Inc.
Ft. Lauderdale, FL

Designers
David Goodwin
Image Works, Inc.

Living Color, Inc.

Client
Coral Square Mall

For this round display, Image Works incorporates stainless steel, copper, perforated aluminum, glass, Plexiglas® acrylic and stained wood. The dolphins, sea horses and coral shells are hand-carved from high-density foam, and the sign's lighting consists of fluorescent, neon and incandescent fixturing. Additionally, the 8-ft.-long aquarium holds live, tropical fish.

Fabricators
Arrow Sign Co.
Oakland, CA

Princeton Welding
Half Moon Bay, CA

Designer
Freedman Tung & Bottomley
San Francisco, CA

Client
The City of Redwood, CA

Fabricated bronze with patina was used to make the area above the neon lighting on this 8 × 30-ft. sign. The white neon "Broadway" is fabricated from aluminum and exposed neon, with a custom perforated-aluminum backing. The illuminated rings are yellow neon and aluminum, and the sign's base is concrete.

Fabricator
National Sign Corp.
Seattle, WA
Designer
Ken Krumpos
National Sign Corp.
Client
Hiway 101 Diner

The "flavor" of this retro diner is reflected in this 10 × 12-ft., double-face pylon display. The "V," which consists of a fabricated cabinet and raceway, is made using an oversized aluminum face with painted graphics and neon. A free-floating, aluminum unit serves as the base for the "Hiway" oval, and the "101" and "Diner" are open-faced channel letters with double-stroke neon.

Fabricator
  Enseicom Signs, Inc.
  Montreal, QC
  Canada
Designer
  Nolin Larosee Design Communications
  Montreal, QC
  Canada
Client
  Casino De Hull
Selling price
  $200,000 (Canadian)

Standing 70-ft. high, this structure consists of 6-in.-diameter galvanized poles welded together to form a 10-ft., half-circle radius. To create the "Casino" logo, the letters are cut out and filled with ⅛-in., white-pigmented Plexiglas® acrylic and internally illuminated with high-output, fluorescent lamps. A full-color matrix — measuring 6 ft. × 14 ft., 8 in. — is installed between the two half circles.

The 5-ft., 6-in.-diameter casino chips are mounted 2 ft. from a concave surface. Each of the six, multilevel chips is illuminated with exposed neon mounted to the circumference and scintillating bulbs on the letter's surface. Red neon is installed behind each chip to create a halo effect.

Fabricator
 Commercial Neon Signs
 Burlington, VT
Designers
 Amey Radcliffe
 Stephanie Salmon
 Gotham City Graphics
 Burlington, VT
Client
 Cosmos Diner
Selling price
 $8,000

The 18-in. neon cup — an open-face channel letter — is designed to catch the attention of passers-by. This display's 24-in.-thick sign cabinet incorporates 22-gauge Color Bond, 3 × 8-ft. sheet metal; a ³⁄₁₆-in.-thick Lexan® face; a horizon-blue neon border; and red neon lettering. 3M™ translucent vinyl is used on the Lexan face panel.

Fabricators
Hunter's Mfg., Inc.
Wilmer, TX

National Neon
Duncanville, TX
Designers
Dan Holzschuh
Landmark Sign Co.
Lewisville, TX

Bob Arnold
Hunter's Mfg., Inc.
Client
Razzoo's
Selling price
$36,963

"Razzoo's" is a triple-pole, illuminated sign that incorporates neon, incandescent lamps, custom cabinets and symbols of 1960s memorabilia. The main cabinet is custom-formed from sheet metal, and includes fade-painted, neon-outlined letters. A square cabinet with neon-outlined letters makes up the secondary sign, while a custom sheet-metal cabinet with (non-chaser) lights is used for the arrow.

Fabricator
Young Electric Sign Co.
Ontario, CA
Designers
Frank Mando and Daniel Adams
Graphic Solutions
San Diego, CA
Client
Montclair Plaza

Measuring 13 ft. 6 in. across and standing 21 ft. high, this single-faced sign features an internally illuminated cabinet, exposed perimeter neon and a stylized, open-channel "M." The sign's davit pole is made of 6-in.-diameter pipe, and forms an 11.69-ft. radius.

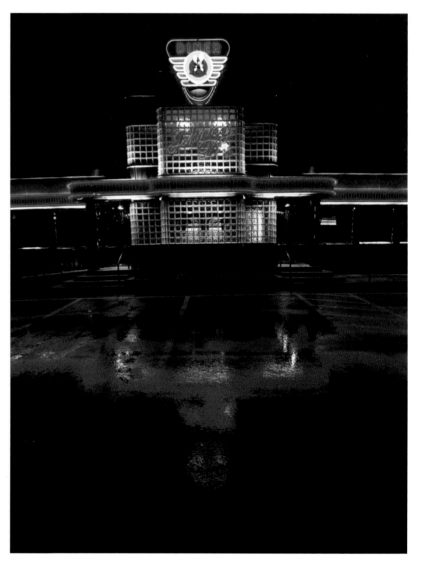

Fabricators
Kullman Industries
Avenel, NJ

USA Signs of America, Inc.
Farmingdale, NY
Designers
Joel Petrocy, Harold Kullman and Mark Blasch
Kullman Industries
Account executive
Robert Kullman
Selling price
$20,400

This diner's foyer utilizes glass block and stainless steel and a sign designed to be an integral part of it. This is achieved with multiple curves and corrugating the mirror-finish stainless steel to frame a two-level, glass-block detail. This creates a perception of depth and soft round corners. The sign projects 18 in. above the roof line. The sign has four levels of depth, and its 3-D structure is enhanced by neon and gradation of color when lit at night. The sign is clipped 4 in. off the wall to make it appear to float. Overall, it extends 30 in. in front of the building to stand out like a medallion. "Johnny D's" has 4-in.-deep, self-contained, single-stroke channel letters, all of which are incorporated into glass block. Black edging around the channel letters adds to the 3-D look.

Fabricator
Hoboken Sign Co.
Hoboken, NJ
Designer
Ray Guzman
Hoboken Sign Co.
Account executive
Renata Guzman

Two sets of 4 × 20-ft. acrylic panels are used for this double-faced sign. The black lettering outline is computer-cut in reverse. All of the artwork, background and letters are hand-cut and applied in reverse. This allows the panel to slide into the box with the face smooth and untouched. The sign had to be retrofitted into an existing sign frame.

Fabricators
  Hunter's Mfg.
  Wilmer, TX

  National Neon
  Duncanville, TX
Designer
  Dan Holzschuh
  Landmark Sign Co.
  Lewisville, TX
Account executive
  Dan Holzschuh
Selling price
  $8,900

This 4 × 20-ft. sign is fabricated from aluminum with channel letters mounted on a skeleton frame. Brillite® neon tubing, France transformers, Peterson P-K housings and 1-Shot lettering enamels are used.

Fabricator
    National Sign Corp.
    Seattle, WA
Designer
    Ken Krumpos
    National Sign Corp.
Selling price
    $8,000

These two single-face exterior displays are approximately 6 ft. 3 in. × 10 ft. The "Grazie" letters are open-face, pan channel letters with double tubes of neon. "Ristorante" and "Italiano" are milled out of the arced aluminum panels and backed up with green acrylic. Neon behind the arced copy provides halo and letter illumination.

Fabricator
National Sign Corp.
Seattle, WA
Designer
Ken Krumpos
National Sign Corp.
Client
Jo Krueger Design

When creating this 2 × 15-ft., single-face, illuminated display, the retail space and its surroundings were taken into consideration. The top layer behind "Jo Krueger" is on a higher plane with a stone-like break in the face going down to the "Interiors" level. Round-head carriage bolts and the "rusted" finish of the "Interiors" portion of the sign contribute to the tech feel. All copy is routed out of the aluminum background with push-through, ½-in. acrylic copy. Diffuser film is laminated to the surface of the copy for illumination through the face and a halo effect. A single tube of white neon runs through the faces.

Fabricator
Young Electric Sign Co.
Ontario, CA

Designers
Frank Mundo
Daniel Adams
Graphic Solutions
San Diego, CA

Client
Donahue Schriber/
Montclair Plaza

This 9-ft.-tall × 19-ft., 6-in.-wide mounted sign is fabricated from perforated metal with solid-metal panel shapes. It has a 9-ft., 6-in. radius that wraps around the building's corner. Exposed perimeter neon is part of the internally illuminated cabinet, and the "M" is an open channel letter. A new building facade provides the sign's background.

Fabricator
T&L Displays
Olympia, WA
Designer
Ken Krumpos
K & Co.
Tacoma, WA
Client
The Oyster House

Reverse, aluminum channel letters are painted satin silver for "The Oyster House." The secondary aluminum cut-out behind the letters is painted blue and employs horizon-blue neon for a halo effect. The oyster is fabricated foam with Fiberglas®. Peach neon illuminates the oyster's mouth, while double-stroke peach neon casts a halo effect onto the building. Double-stroke horizon-blue neon is used for the building's border, and the building's wave graphic is blue neon with a scripting transformer. The sign measures 6 × 10 ft.

Fabricator
ARTeffects, Inc.
Bloomfield, CT

Designers
John Everett
Paul and Mary Frishmann
New England Design
Mansfield, CT

Lawrin Rosen
ARTeffects, Inc.

Client
International at Foxwoods

Carved Sign Foam® high-density urethane with an enamel finish makes up the base of this display. The sign cabinet comprises .060 aluminum with light panels on the top and bottom to wash the carvings. All the face graphics were created using the GerberEDGE®. Two layers of painted, ½-in. Sintra™ expanded PVC sheet serve as the sign's backing.

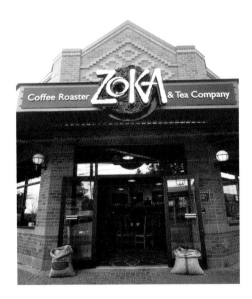

Fabricator
National Sign Corp.
Seattle, WA

Designers
Walsh & Assoc.
Seattle, WA

Ken Krumpos
National Sign Corp.

Client
Zoka

Selling price
$8,000

Layers and subtle lighting create a "neighborhood coffeehouse" environment with this 3 × 12-ft. single-face display. The background panel is aluminum with surface-applied, ½-in. acrylic letters. "Aztec Coin" is a carved Sign Foam® piece with an airbrushed patina that floats off the background with a red halo. The "Zoka" letters are cut out of aluminum and offset from the coin. White neon placed behind the letters creates a halo effect.

Fabricators
Jayco Signs, Inc.
Maitland, FL

Gulf State Plastics, Inc.
Deland, FL
Selling price
$14,000

The logo cabinet for this sign is 10 × 12 ft., and the extruded aluminum cabinet is 2 × 12 ft. The faces are backsprayed Lexan® polycarbonate with fluorescent illumination. The logo cabinet is fabricated in an irregular shape with triple-embossed Lexan polycarbonate for special effects.

Fabricator
National Sign Corp.
Seattle, WA
Designer
Ken Krumpos
National Sign Corp.
Client
Wild Salmon

By employing layers and indirect lighting, the fabricator creates a unique feel in this upper-end fish market. "Wild Salmon" is routed out of ¼-in. aluminum, which blends and becomes the background of the milled-out "Seafood Market." A fluorescent lamp illuminates the secondary copy from behind, while a tube of horizon-blue neon bathes up behind the "Wild Salmon" onto the fish graphic. The orbital fish behind the blue fish is on a second plane for surface enrichment.

Fabricator
Independent Sign Co.
Denver, CO
Designer
Smith, Nelson & Oatis
Denver, CO
Account executive
Bob Sibilia
Selling price
$22,000

This 5 × 15-ft., all-aluminum projecting sign combines recessed and exposed neon. The sign is designed to complement the architectural scheme of Larimer Square.

Fabricators
  Sign Crafters
  San Marcos, TX

  Morris Signs
  New Braunfels, TX
Designers
  Bender Wells Clark Design
  San Antonio, TX

  Scott Vaughan
  Sign Crafters
Account executive
  Scott Vaughan
Selling price
  $42,000

This 16 × 30-ft. sign is constructed of aluminum. Its specially milled urethane face creates a unique water effect when water flows out of the top of the sign and ripples down the sign face. The backlit, reverse-channel flags light the ripples. Water jets hit the beveled bottom edge to create a "rolling wave" that makes the fountain appear to float. Unfortunately, given Texas' drought conditions, no water currently flows through the sign.

Fabricator
    Image Works, Inc.
    Ashland, VA
Designer
    David Goodwin
    Image Works, Inc.

This sign's distinctive nautical theme reflects the nearby ocean. The project was approached more as sculpture than as signage. The all-aluminum display includes acrylic and exposed neon. Special features include illumination all the way to the ground, and pilings and rope emphasize the nautical theme. The overall size is 13 ft. 3 in. × 25 ft.

Fabricator
Sign Productions, Inc.
Cedar Rapids, IA
Designer
Doug Stancel
Sign Productions, Inc.
Account executive
Steve Allsop
Selling price
$15,000

This 7 ft., 6-in. × 14 ft., 10-in. single-face sign incorporates acrylic blocks backlit with fluorescent tubes. The "P" and "Intuit" are Plexiglas® acrylic-faced channel letters illuminated with neon. The rest of the copy is non-illuminated, reverse channel letters, although the background is lit at night. The column tops are Plexiglas acrylic lit with fluorescent tubes.

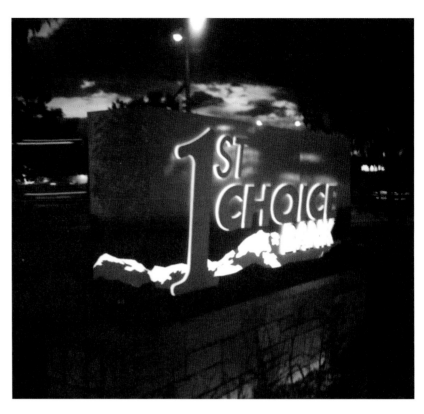

Fabricator
  Shaw Sign & Awning, Inc.
  Ft. Collins, CO
Designer
  Dallas Griffin
  Shaw Sign & Awning, Inc.
Account executive
  Kevin Callihan

Approximately 11 ft. wide and 5 ft. tall, this sign features a routed, painted aluminum cabinet with ¾-in. push-through text. The unusual fabrication is characterized by the mountain-range graphic that illuminates on all four sides.

Fabricator
   ARTeffects, Inc.
   Bloomfield, CT
Designer
   Hal Wood
   ARTeffects, Inc.
Client
   Grolier

A fabricated, .125 aluminum-plate finished with Zolatone paint is used for the main body of this display. Push-through copy of ½-in. acrylic was heated for a polished finish. Casocryl's day/night (black during the day/white during the night) acrylic is also used. The "G" is a channel letter.

Fabricator
ARTeffects, Inc.
Bloomfield, CT
Designers
Lawrin Rosen
Hal Wood
ARTeffects, Inc.
Client
Hastings Hotel

The main cabinet of this sign is made of routed, .125 aluminum-plate faces. For the lower portion of the sign, ¼-in. brushed-aluminum plate letters are attached to a "wash"-lit cove backer of fabricated aluminum. The round PVC pipe uprights and the .125 aluminum-plate base are finished to resemble cast concrete.

Fabricator
Gordon Sign Co.
Denver, CO
Designer
Lance Jackson & Assoc.
Denver, CO
Client
Club Sports Intl.
Selling price
$21,000

Here is a 12 × 10-ft., double-face sign with a separate logo cabinet inside that's rotated 30°. Further, this sign features ⅛-in. aluminum, no visible seams or fasteners, a pearl-haze painted finish, and non-illuminated, reverse-channel, chrome letters. The logo cabinet has polycarbonate faces with vinyl overlay.

Fabricator
Gordon Sign Co.
Denver, CO
Designer
C.W. Fentress
J.H. Bradburn & Assoc., PC
Denver, CO
Account executive
Steve Wisian
Selling price
$40,000

The structure for this sign is made of
bent and formed 6-in.-diameter tube
with steel-plate diamonds. The logo
functions as a 5-ft.-diameter clock; the
purple letters are vinyl, and the clock
face is screen printed. Reverse, pan-
channel letters are illuminated with
overlays on curved stringers. The sign's
overall size is 36½ ft. tall, 23½ ft. wide
and 4½ ft. deep.

Fabricator
Gordon Sign Co.
Denver, CO
Designer
Ron Hull
Gordon Sign Co.
Client
EAS
Selling price
$19,000

A 2-ft. 6-in.-diameter column with a free-form aluminum graphic and aluminum address channel letters are incorporated in this structure. The column is flanked by two 7 ft. 3-in. curved wings of textured aluminum and push-through, ½-in., clear acrylic overlaid with vinyl. Additionally, this display boasts a smooth, concrete base; a textured, aluminum framework around the wings; and a Wrisco column cap.

Fabricator
Arrow Sign Co.
Oakland, CA
Designer
Charlie Stroud
Arrow Sign Co.
Client
Abbott Laboratories

This 3 ft. 9-in.-tall × 17 ft., 9-in.-wide design employs fabricated aluminum with routed grooves and rolled frame to match the building's entry. The main copy is 1-in. acrylic push-through letters with brushed aluminum overlay, while the secondary copy is flat, cut-out aluminum with flood illumination.

Fabricator
Gordon Sign Co.
Denver, CO
Designer
Ron Hull
Gordon Sign Co.
Account executive
Steve Wisian
Selling price
$30,000

Key to this hotel sign's design, are a four-faced, projecting clock features central movement, white neon illumination, a raised border around the face and cut-out aluminum numerals. The sign structure itself measures 4 ft. 5 in. × 11 ft. and includes fabricated reverse-channel letters overlayed with gold-anodized brushed aluminum. On all four sign faces relief elements are fabricated from aluminum square tube, and painted to match the environment.

Fabricator
Creative Neon Works Inc.
Dartmouth, NS
Canada
Designer
Creative Neon Works, Inc.

Self-contained channel letters, exposed neon and cut-out Lexan® characters make up this 13 × 18-ft., original-logo sign. Carved, high-density styrofoam that has been fiberglassed and hand-painted is used for the 12 ft.-long, 8-in.-thick shark. According to the client, the sign has "made his business." In fact, the cost of the sign was reclaimed within four weeks of its installation.

Fabricator
Ultraneon Sign Co.
San Diego, CA
Designers
Panda Mgt.
South Pasadena, CA

Dave Green
Ultraneon Sign Co.
Account executive
John Y. Hadaya
Selling price
$17,000

Located in an upscale shopping mall, this restaurant uses sign visibility, curb appeal and a Panda bear logo to project its oriental theme. The 19 × 10-ft. storefront system includes arch- and open-channel letters, a 4-ft.-diameter, formed-acrylic ball, exposed neon and awnings. All brackets feature aluminum construction.

Fabricator
   Ultraneon Sign Co.
   San Diego, CA
Designer
   Graphic Solutions
   San Diego, CA
Account executive
   John Y. Hadaya
Selling price
   $12,000

Dark-green, patina-finished filigree is the heart of this bold 3 × 21-ft. salon display. Highly visible open pan-channel letters with exposed neon facilitate name and brand recognition, while the tag line uses a more subdued routed face with reverse illumination. In addition, a low-voltage lamp, placed inside 3-D metal flowers, creates a nighttime sparkling effect.

Fabricator
    National Sign Corp.
    Seattle, WA
Designer
    Kay Rice
    National Sign Corp.
Client
    World Wrapps Restaurant
Selling price
    $15,000

The sign's 3 × 12-ft., double-sided panel incorporates a random or-bital finish, a halo-green background effect and two offset layers of copy. Open-pan channel letters with exposed, horizon-blue neon are used for the "World Wrapps" lettering, and orbs with surface-applied neon wrap around the panel from front to back.

Attached to the sign's 3-D, aluminum-disc globe are rolled-aluminum continents and surface-applied neon. Skeleton neon runs up and around all four sides of the cabinet; a full-color, 3M™ Scotchprint graphic provides additional global appeal.

Fabricator
Arrow Sign Co.
Oakland, CA
Designer
Charlie Stroud
Arrow Sign Co.
Client
Yoshi's Japanese Restaurant
and Jazz Club

To most effectively display this unique logo, Arrow Sign Co., Oakland, CA, uses a 5 × 5-ft. rolled-aluminum background panel, painted red. For the copy, Arrow uses aluminum FCO, standing-off from the red background. Other sign features include a rolled, square tube with FCO aluminum copy; exposed neon border tubing; and flood illumination via three, low-voltage fixtures.

Fabricator
Neon Products
(Div. of The Jim Pattison Sign Group)
Richmond, BC
Canada
Designer
Neon Products
Client
Waldorf Hotel (BC, Canada)

Not to be confused with the Astoria in New York (NY), this Waldorf Hotel is located in British Columbia. The dramatic, colorful sign incorporates vinyl and painted graphics on Plexiglas® acrylic faces, as well as Cooley Brite 4048 forest-green flexible-face background material.

Interestingly, the graphics were created to cover the building's two existing cabinets: the 32-ft. 2-in. × 4-ft. 8-in., vertical, double-faced, primary cabinet, as well as the 8 × 15-ft., rounded, secondary cabinet. For the retrofit, both cabinets and their retainers were repainted to Pantone 3435 dark green.

Fabricator
National Sign Corp.
Seattle, WA
Designer
Ken Krumpos
National Sign Corp.
Client
Juba Juice/Food Restaurant

The 3-ft. 6-in. × 17-ft., single-faced, interior display has 2-in.-deep, acrylic "Juba" letters with acrylic returns, illuminated from behind. Juba's orb is a fabricated cabinet with a routed aluminum face and an accent ring of horizon-blue neon. The secondary copy is routed, push-through, ½-in. acrylic on a raceway that bathes the "reeds," which are offset from the background facade.

Fabricator
ARTeffects, Inc.
Bloomfield, CT
Designer
Sonalyst Studios
Waterford, CT
Client
Mohegan Territory Casino

Epoxy-coated Styrofoam plastic foam, cup-led with plywood bracing, is used for the top portion of this sign. The map is a GerberEDGE® thermal-transfer print, spliced orange-peel-style around the cup's perimeter.

"Mohegan" consists of hammered, "aged," halo letters on an oxidized, faux-green-patina aluminum background. "Territory" is a sign cabinet with an oxidized "rust" background.

Fabricator
National Sign Corp.
Seattle, WA
Designer
Kay Rice
National Sign Corp.
Client
World Wrapps Restaurant
Selling price
$12,000

For this restaurant's 5 × 6-ft. single-face display, National Sign Corp., Seattle, WA, uses a unique combination of texture, dimension and neon. For example, the background panel behind the copy has a random orbital finish with two pegged-off copy layers; the "World Wrapps" letters are open-pan channel letters with exposed, horizon-blue neon. Halo-green illumination is used for behind the background panel.

A spun aluminum disc with rolled aluminum continents and surface-applied neon make up the sign's 3-D globe. The orbs floating around the panel are surface-applied neon.

Fabricator
ARTeffects, Inc.
Bloomfield, CT
Designers
Lawrin Rosen (sign)
ARTeffects, Inc.

Rainwater Design (logo)
Hartford, CT

Niemitz Design Group
(architecture)
Selling price
$4,200

"MAX" — the predominant copy in this restaurant sign — comprises open-faced stainless-steel channel letters and exposed, clear, 12mm red neon. "Downtown" is fabricated using a routed brass oval and ½-in. clear push-thru letters, outlined in black.

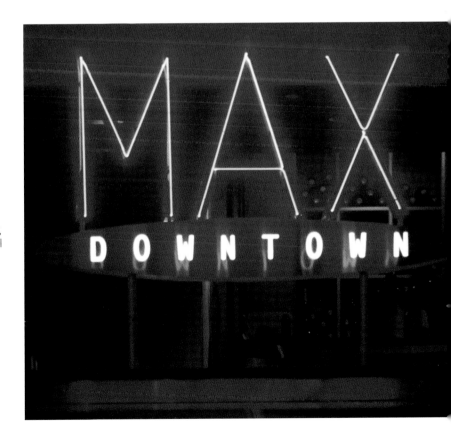

Fabricator
National Sign Corp.
Seattle, WA
Designer
Design Partnership
Portland, OR
Selling price
$130,000

In Washington Square's Summit Food Court, four sign types are used: a single-faced, 8 × 25-ft., interior wall display; a single-faced 8 × 25-ft. exterior wall display; 11-ft.-high, double-faced, non-illuminated sentry signs; and double-faced, illuminated 1 ft. × 3 ft. × 6-in. restroom and directional signs.

For the primary interior sign, the "Summit" letters are fabricated channel letters with acrylic faces and ½-in. clear-acrylic panels embedded in the letter returns. Half-in. clear acrylic is also used for the mountain shape, which features a screen-printed photo image on the second surface and an underneath light source to illuminate the mountain edge. Behind the "Summit" copy is a cabinet with an acrylic face and perforated metal top, allowing for a low-key illuminated pattern. This cabinet also acts as an electrical raceway. Rolled aluminum is used for the flatware and large plate graphics, and the smaller plate conceals a neon tube that affords a halo effect. "Food Collection" is routed out of an aluminum background. The fabricated aluminum wordbox is build on a gentle arc and pegged off the other portion of the sign.

Similar in appearance to the interior sign, the exterior display comprises open-face pan-channel letters with double-tube horizon blue neon. The letters are backed with separate illuminated cabinets that have acrylic faces and stripes. Again, "Food Collection" is routed out of an aluminum-faced cabinet.

All sentry signs are fabricated aluminum shapes with screen-printed ½-in. clear-acrylic graphic panels. Cone-shaped bases are carved high-density urethane with a polyurethane finish. Rolled and brushed aluminum is used to fabricate the spoon and fork end pieces.

Finally, restroom and directional signs feature a laser-cut aluminum background; a ¾-in., clear-acrylic panel with sandblasted stripes sandwiched between; and a decorative, perforated brushed-aluminum panel. An indirect lightsource provides edge lighting.

Fabricator
Ultraneon Sign Co.
San Diego, CA
Designer
Dave Green
Ultraneon Sign Co.
Account executive
John Y. Hadaya
Selling price
$14,000

Rocco's Hair Design's (Horton Plaza, San Diego, CA) primary identification sign — a 1 × 6-ft. storefront sign — is fabricated using reverse pan-channel letters, white-neon halo illumination and mirror-finish chrome faces. A ruby-red exposed-neon swash complements the original logo design, and also illuminates the "Hair Design" lettering.

Patterned after the storefront sign, the shop's ceiling-mounted, 5 × 4-ft., aluminum-blade, double-faced sign, is installed in a busy walkway near the salon. As such, it uses skeleton neon letters and graphics for maximum exposure.

The third sign in this system — a non-illuminated, double-faced, 6 × 5-ft. scissor icon — is mounted on the second mall level. It has an aluminum body with polyurethane copy and graphics.

Fabricator
ARTeffects, Inc.
Bloomfield, CT
Designers
William Johnson
ARTeffects, Inc.

Karl Norton and Paul Frishman
New England Design
Mansfield, CT
Account executive
William Johnson

Casino signs for the Racebook at Foxwoods are fabricated using translucent vinyl graphics, dimensional halo letters, and both direct and indirect lighting. The signs' horses are carved from high-density urethane, then bronzed and antiqued.

Fabricators
California Neon Products
San Diego, CA

Moran Canvas
San Diego, CA

Designer
J. Newbold Assoc.
New York, NY

Account executive
Mike Bates

Selling price
$124,000

Horton Plaza's toy store, FAO Schwarz, features a main identification sign with 7-ft. aluminum blocks mounted on a truss. These blocks — which thematically reinforce the store's identity — incorporate ⅜-in. aluminum graphics appliqués, as well as exposed neon.

Canvas awnings, interior neon ceiling sculptures and cove lighting are also used throughout the store's sign system.

Fabricator
Superior Sign Systems
Vacaville, CA
Designer
Sayed Aslami
Sacramento, CA
Account executive
Jerry Wyman
Selling price
$12,000

Individual open-face channel letters are used for Jack London Cinema's primary sign. These letters comprise Tecnolux neon, mounted atop reverse-channel, polished-aluminum, halo-lit letters. A Lexan face and an exposed-neon border inside the channel are used for the 8 × 6-ft. theatre marquis. The cinema's stripes are exposed neon inside a channel, and curved around the tower.

Fabricator
  ARTeffects, Inc.
  Bloomfield, CT

Designers
  John Everett
  Paul and Mary Frishmann
  New England Design
  Mansfield, CT

  Lawrin Rosen, Hal Wood,
  Jane Turbacuski
  ARTeffects, Inc.

Client
  Festival Buffet at
  Foxwoods Casino

Feast your eyes on these signs: They're made of Sign Foam® high-density urethane and Styrofoam plastic foam, and incorporate a delicious array of carved details. In addition, the signs feature illuminated cabinets with wash lighting, top and bottom; GerberEDGE® thermal-transfer printed graphics; and backers made of layered, ½-in., Sintra™ expanded PVC sheet.

Fabricator
White Way Sign
Chicago, IL
Designer
Plancom Design Team
Chicago, IL
Client
Trump Hotels and Casino
Resorts/Barden Development/
The Casinos at Buffington Harbor

The grand entrance sign at the Casinos at Buffington Harbor is made of 90-ft.-high towers and large, rotating spheres that project beams of white light into the night sky. "Buffington" consists of 10-ft.-high channel letters, each with a red Plexiglas® acrylic face, four tubes of red-neon interior illumination, and single tube of perimeter yellow neon. "Harbor" and "Casinos" are channel letters with red Plexiglas acrylic, illuminated via double tubes of red neon. The twin towers' vertical column covers consist of 12 rows of single-tube bromo-blue neon with a three-point mechanical flasher. Horizontal column covers each use six turquoise neon rings with a three-point mechanical flasher. Pedestals next to the main sign display the "Trump Casino" and "Majestic Star Casino" logos, made of red-Plexiglas acrylic channel letters internally illuminated with red neon. Above these logos are star and mermaid figures, each of which is made with dimensional foam.

The use of neon continues into the pavilion, unifying the casinos' exterior and interior signage. Illuminated overhead directionals are fabricated metal enclosures with interior fluorescent illumination. Turquoise neon accent rings wrap around conical cylinders capped with Tivoli red lamps. The interior signs' perimeters and copy are push-through acrylic.

Fabricator
National Sign Corp.
Seattle, WA
Designer
TRA Graphic Design
Seattle, WA
Client
Emerald Downs
Selling price
$200,000

At the main entrance to the Emerald Downs horseracing facility, you'll find 11-ft.-high, self-contained channel letters. Their letter faces are white with a yellow vinyl overlay, illuminated internally with a grid of neon, and 15-in. returns painted teal to match the building. Emerald Downs' wayfinding system includes a variety of secondary displays. All are non-illuminated, and incorporate different planes of painted/finished aluminum to create visual interest.

Fabricators
  Acolite Claud United
  Hialeah, FL

  Graphic Systems Inc.
  Orlando, FL
Designer
  Tom Graboski Assoc., Inc.
  Coral Gables, FL
Client
  Dadeland Station/Berkowitz
  Development
Selling price
  $5,000-55,000/sign

Dadeland Station's tenants are identified by signage arranged in a vertical format. Specifically, the system orients visitors to the center; directs the visitors to the appropriate parking level in the six-story, 1500-car garage; and guides them across the bridge to the correct retail store. All interior garage signs identify tenants by name and parking deck/bridge level.

Included here are photos of three of the site's signs, including Dadeland Station's primary, 20-ft.-tall, 200-sq.-ft., double-faced pylon sign (top). Channel letters are used for Dadeland's logo, and boat-shaped, flexible-face, metal-halide illuminated panels are used for each of the five tenant signs.

Also depicted here is Dadeland Station's 20-ft.-tall, 120-sq.-ft., double-faced, secondary-entry pylon sign. The pole is set back from the road and sidewalk to clear underground utilities. The graphic is cantilevered outward to meet the county's 7-ft.-setback sign-code requirement.

The smallest of the three signs is wall-mounted, double-faced and serves as a parking garage entry ID sign. The "P" is internally illuminated, measures 3 ft. in diameter, and features skeleton neon.

Fabricator
Imperial Sign Corp.
Port Coquitlam, BC
Canada

Designer
Sally Emerson
Raven Interior Design Inc.
West Vancouver, BC
Canada

Client
8 Rinks Ice-Sports Centre

Selling price
$150,000 (Canadian)

Slick design and bright colors abound in this sign system. 8-Rinks' primary sign (top left) measures 25 ft. tall × 23 ft. 3 in. wide, features an all-aluminum structure and incorporates a 16 × 144-matrix Adtronics 7.5-watt-lamp message display. "8-Rinks" and "Home of the Canucks" are channel letters, and the series of horizontal red lines are illuminated channel shapes. Encircling the aqua disk in the sign's center is a turquoise neon border. This sign weighs approximately 6,000 lbs. and is through-bolted onto an aluminum-clad cinder-block wall.

The 19-ft.-tall, 8-ft.-wide, aluminum and vinyl sign (top right) identifies the tenants in the ice complex. To expedite tenant name changes, the sign has cut-out copy attached to the background.

Like the multi-tenant sign, the other two signs depicted here — the Canucks Training Centre sign and the Entrance sign — also use all-aluminum construction and vinyl graphics.

Fabricators
Display Solutions SA (PTY) Ltd.
Cape Town, South Africa

Union Structural Eng.
Cape Town, South Africa
Designer
Gahwiler & Assoc.
Cape Town, South Africa

Located at the main entrance to Tyger Valley Shopping Centre — a major regional shopping center in Cape Town, South Africa — this translucent white sign was designed to stand out against the blue African sky. The 15m-tall structure incorporates 100 × 100mm, hollow, steel sections, with 50 × 50mm weld-mesh panels fitted in between; these carry the Alucobond-clad 8 × 1m electronic message board.

Underneath the sign is 3m-deep pool of water; protruding through it are ceramic-tiled concrete foundations, on which both pylon legs rest. Powered uplights housed within these legs dramatically illuminate the sign, making it a highly visible landmark in the area. A water spillway behind the sign adds sound to the structure, and further enhances its visual excitement.

Fabricator
   Ad-Art Electronic Sign Corp.
   Stockton, CA
Designer
   Tony Ortega
   Ad-Art Electronic Sign Corp.
Account executive
   Ralph Cundiff
Selling price
   $225,000

Standing 45 ft. high and 19½ ft. wide, this double-faced pylon display incorporates a welded square tube upper structure over multiple (eight) concrete columns. The 8-ft. "W" logos are metal channel letters internally illuminated with white neon; their faces are teal 3M™ film. These logos are diffused and separated with perforated aluminum screen material.

Each of the 2 ft. 3-in. reverse-channel "Weberstown" letters is painted black and pegged off a painted metal background. They are indirectly illuminated with white neon for a halo effect.

Finally, the sign's 8 × 12-ft., 65,000-color Ad-Art Electronic Sign Corp. Infovision electronic graphics display has a 64 × 96 matrix, with lamps 1½-in. o.c. In addition to producing full-color graphics and messages, the display has video capability.

Fabricator
ARTeffects, Inc.
Bloomfield, CT
Designer
William Johnson
ARTeffects, Inc.
Account executive
William Johnson
Selling price
$8,700

A Sign Comp extrusion and routed aluminum faces are used in this bank's pylon sign. The sign's LED time-and-temperature display is manufactured by Voltarc.

Fabricator
Alvey's Signs, Inc.
Evansville, IN
Designers
Juan Lopez-Bonilla and Dan Stewart
Louisville, KY
Account executive
Marilyn Rumsey
Selling price
$300,000 (14 banks)

This pylon is part of a multi-sign system for this bank, and also part of a much larger corporate identity system designed for a 14-branch bank corporation. By using the design pictured here, the corporation portrays a unified look, even though some of the branches maintain their own names.

Among the branches, pylons like this one stand from 20-29 ft. tall, are internally illuminated, and use a steel and aluminum welded frame, clad with .125 aluminum. Each bank name and logo is routed using a System 600, and backed with computer-cut, matching acrylic push-through letters. Bold red and black acrylic light bars embellish the sides of the cabinets.

Fabricator
Sign Productions, Inc.
Cedar Rapids, IA
Designer
Doug Stancel
Marion, IA
Client
First Trust Bank
Selling price
$30,000

Good design and clean fabrication can be credited for this bank's sign. Routed-aluminum cabinets and faces and illuminated fascia fixtures are used in this double-faced display. A message center mounted to a custom brick-and-block base is also featured.

Fabricator
ARTeffects, Inc.
Bloomfield, CT
Designer
William Johnson
ARTeffects, Inc.
Account executive
William Johnson
Selling price
$10,000

A unique yellow brick pedestal is key to this sign's design; it mimics the window shapes of the nearby building. Fabricated ⅛-in. aluminum plate cabinet and cornices, polycarbonate faces, an opaque background and translucent letters complete the structure. The LED time-and-temperature display is manufactured by Voltarc.

Fabricators
California Neon Products
San Diego, CA

Cinnabar (Armored Car)
Hollywood, CA

Display Ad Intl. (LED Displays)
Las Vegas, NV

Vegas Steel (Steel Beam Support)
Las Vegas, NV

Jakes Crane & Rigging (Crane Service)
Las Vegas, NV

Designers
Dan Avallone, Glenn Stanton
California Neon Products

Dailey & Assoc. Adv.
Los Angeles, CA

Client
Display Ad Intl./IGT — Gaming

Selling price
$2.5 million

You can bet that people at Las Vegas' (NV) McCarren Airport notice this sign. Suspended between columns in the airport's baggage claim area, it measures 10 ft. high × 11 ft. 6 in. deep × 60 ft. long.

The sign's full-color LED displays, manufactured by Display Ad Intl., Las Vegas, simulate slot-machine operation as the illuminated pull handle is lowered. Real-time satellite links to IGT Headquarters are used to update the current progressive jackpot amount on this and other IGT games throughout the world.

To ensure the sign's realism, sign-fabricator California Neon Products, San Diego, CA, used a full-sized armored car, manufactured by Cinnabar, Hollywood, CA. Fabricated from aluminum and fiberglass, the armored car has operational running lights and is filled with cash.

The entire display is mounted on a structural steel-beam support, and comprises a tubular steel frame and aluminum cabinetry. Skeleton neon is used for the secondary sign.

Fabricator
Neon Products
(Div. of The Jim Pattison Sign Group)
Richmond, BC
Canada
Designer
Sheena Gibbs
Neon Products
Client
Paladin's Pub

This double-faced, projecting illuminated display measures 3 ft. in diameter × 10 in. deep, and has a black cabinet and retainer. In addition, the sign features a 3-ft. × 2-ft. 9-in. routed panel backed with Plexiglas® acrylic and reverse-cut vinyl. Some sign-face details are painted, including the ½-in. blue semi-circular lines above and below "Neighborhood Pub."

The sign's arrow is white paint on sheet metal, with a horizon-blue neon outline. Its time-and-temperature unit measures 18 × 48 in., and features 12-in.-high red LED characters.

Fabricator
Signature Signs, Inc.
Newbury Park, CA
Designer
Scott Biley
Signature Signs, Inc.
Client
Thousand Oaks Auto Mall
Selling price
$165,000

The 20-ft.-tall × 30-ft.-wide display, created for Thousand Oaks Auto Mall, uses galvanized sheet metal covered with urethane foam, stucco and tile trim; pole covers; reverse-bronze Muntz Metal letters; and an American Electronic Sign time-and-temperature unit. Twelve varieties of flowering plants are featured in and around the sign; they're watered via a computerized irrigation drip system.

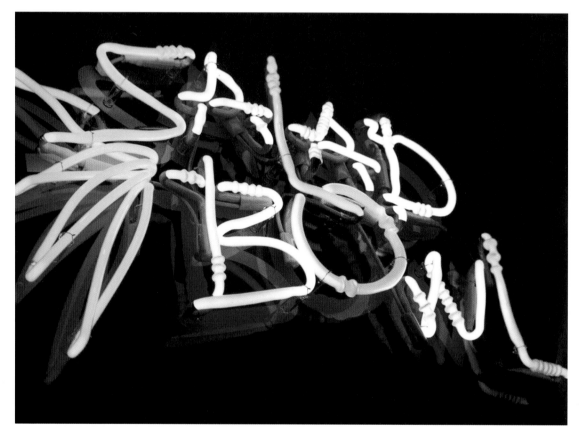

Fabricator
ARTeffects, Inc.
Bloomfield, CT
Designer
Lawrin Rosen
ARTeffects, Inc.
Account executive
Lawrin Rosen
Selling price
$2,100

Yellow, purple and green 12mm argon tubing illuminates this restaurant logo. A black acrylic backer ensures that the multicolored letters stand out.

Fabricator
Independent Sign Co.
Denver, CO
Designer
Smith, Nelson & Oatis
Denver, CO
Account executive
Bob Sibilia
Selling price
$18,000

This 5 × 12-ft. aluminum sign is a combination of recessed and exposed neon and scintillating incandescents. In a incandescents step-by-step animation cycle, the bottle rises to fill the mug with beer. A foam "head" is added to make the sign as effective as the real stuff.

Fabricator
  Neon Latitudes
  Eugene, OR
Designers
  Annie Fulkerson and Ron Weil
  Eugene, OR

  Neal Conner
  Neon Latitudes
Account executive
  Neal Conner
Selling price
  $12,000

The main sign in this natural foods store is 10 ft. tall and 20 ft. wide. The letters are attached at various depths to create a "staggered" look. Green and turquoise tubes on either side of this main sign draw attention to two camel enclosures illuminated by a "halo" of green light.

Fabricators
Landmark Sign Co.
Lewisville, TX

National Neon
Duncanville, TX
Designer
Dan Holzschuh
Landmark Sign Co.
Account executive
Dan Holzschuh
Selling price
$6,000

To match this restaurant's old architecture and decor, its 3 × 8-ft. sign is made to look like it has been around for a while.

Fabricator
Neon Pro Signs
Masson-Angers, QC
Canada

Designers
Chantal Baril
Canadian Museum of Civilisations
Hull, QC
Canada

Rene Giroux
Neon Pro Signs

Client
Canadian Postal Museum

Selling price
$12,000 (Canadian)

The new Canadian Postal Museum in Hull, ON, near Ottawa, boasts this main-entrance sign. The display has a 7 × 14-ft. Signcomp retro frame with white Ultralon™ 4 flexible-face fabric. To create the center, a reverse channel is made with the client's logo in 24-gauge steel with silver-metallic paint and a white neon halo. Cobalt blue and ruby-red neon accents are visible on the front. All electrical equipment and channel letters are mounted on a ⅛-in. aluminum plate.

Both stamps are produced on the GerberEDGE® thermal-transfer printer. The red stamp is mounted on ¼-in. white Sintra™ expanded PVC sheet. The window graphic elements are made from 3M™ 2-mil vinyl with frosted vinyl by 3M applied on the second side of the glass.

Fabricators
Dave Figula
Figula Neon
Scranton, PA

Allen Figula
Figula Designs
Glen Hope, PA
Designers
Dave and Allen Figula
Client
Rocky's Lounge
Selling Price
$11,000

The Figula brothers designed this sign to last with a steel-frame marquee and changeable copy. The upper section has aluminum 1½-in.-sq. angle grids. Also featured are animated Lexan™ blocks with red neon; these move at 1-second intervals. The overall size of the sign is 14 ft. inside × 18 ft. high.

Red trim lines the building at the top level and white trim accents the bottom level. The upper level has 36-in., cut, black acrylic with a gray airbrush fade, and is backlit with a double line in red neon. Additionally, the side of the building has matching channel letters. A small matching marquee is placed over the fire exits. The front and side of the building have small marquees with 1½ in. sq. aluminum grid patterns and Lexan block. The building also has matching 48-in.-high, 62-in.-wide, marquee-size roof lines that are lit from behind with purple neon.

Fabricator
National Sign Corp.
Seattle, WA
Designer
Kay Rice
National Sign Corp.
Client
World Wrapps Restaurant
Selling price
$8,000

Texture, dimension and neon are employed in this 3 × 15-ft., single-face display to grab your attention. Random orbital finishes with two offset copy layers back up the panels, while the "World Wrapps" letters are open-pan channel with exposed horizon-blue neon. Halo-green neon highlights the background panels. The 3-D globe is a spun aluminum disc with rolled-aluminum continents and neon applied to the surface. For a truly global feel, the orbs floating around the panel wrap from front to back with surface-applied neon, and the globe background is halo-green neon.

Fabricators
Hunters Mfg.
Wilmer, TX

National Neon
Duncanville, TX
Designer
Dan Holzschuh
Landmark Sign Co.
Lewisville, TX
Account executive
Dan Holzschuh
Selling price
$7,500

To promote the historic district in which it is located, this restaurant carries an old-style sign that includes exposed neon on painted graphics. Fabricators used 1-Shot enamels and Brillite® neon tubing.

Fabricator
Neon Products
(Div. of The Jim Pattison Sign Group)
Richmond, BC
Canada

Designer
Dennis Calder
Neon Products

Open channel letters and exposed neon really "perk up" this sign. The "the" employs gold neon; the words "Java Hut" are open channel letters illuminated with red neon; and the insides of the letters are painted in yellow with the outsides painted green. To create the 6-ft. palm tree, Neon Products used painted sheet-metal and added green neon to represent the leaves and gold neon for the yellow trunk. The raceway is painted blue with a single line of medium-blue neon and beige on the bottom.

Fabricator
Neon-Line Werbedesign GmbH
Vienna, Austria

Designer
Dusty Sprengnagel
Neon-Line Werbedesign Gmbll

Client
Classic Rock Cafe

This sign measures 280 × 160cm (9 × 4½ ft.) and has an aluminum frame and acrylic front. The background is screen printed and then backlit with fluorescent tubes. The lettering is neon-outlined and mounted on 10mm flat acrylic; the letters reaching over the case are supported by a construction. The sign advertises the Classic Rock Cafe, which is located on a boat anchored on the Danube Canal.

Fabricators
Tobey Archer Studio
Ft. Lauderdale, FL

Mer-Vac
Dania, FL
Designer
Tobey Archer
Tobey Archer Studio
Account executive
Tobey Archer
Selling price
$35,000

Atlantic Illuminations Quartet I, II, III and IV, a bas-relief sculpture created for Florida Atlantic University, is constructed of neon and paper on white Lucite™ acrylic. Each of the sculpture's four segments, enclosed in clear Lucite acrylic, measures 4 ft. × 4 ft. × 5 in. and is installed on an 11 × 53-ft. lobby wall. This photo groups the four segments together. According to the fabricators, the sculpture represents water and landscape forms found in the area.

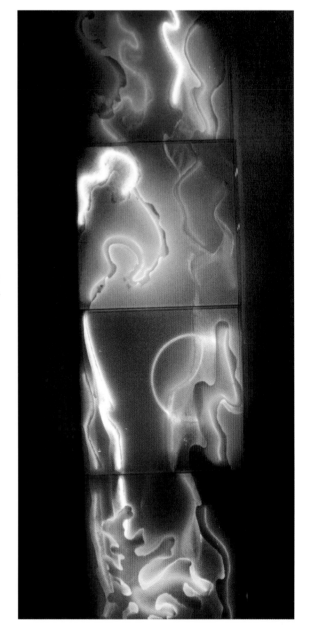

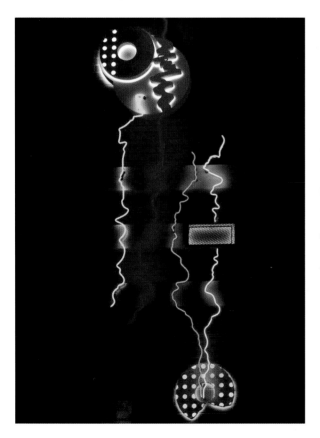

Fabricator
Neon Latitudes
Eugene, OR
Designer
Neal Conner
Neon Latitudes
Account executive
Neal Conner

This 6 × 18-ft.-tall, wall-mounted sculpture features basic sheetmetal components with two polished aluminum discs — one at the top and the other at the bottom. The Tecnolux tubes used for the exposed neon colors are bent in three separate dimensions.

Fabricator
Neon Knights, Inc.
Baltimore, MD
Designer
Marsha D. Lidard
Neon Knights, Inc.
Account cxcoutivcs
Marsha D. Lidard
Arthur Higgins

The 8-ft. palm trees in this sign are made of deep-green and yellow neon, and the waves are flo-blue and white neon. The seagulls are 6500 white, while the sun utilizes orange and yellow neon. The entire scene, mounted onto a painted wooden shadow box, is displayed on a wall, where it is powered by two 15/30mA, two 12/30mA and one 9000/30mA transformers.

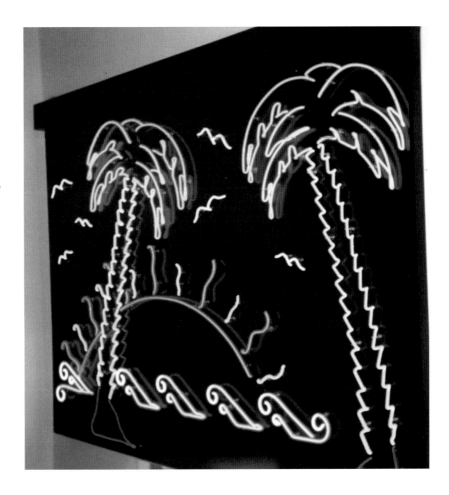

Fabricator
Neon Knights, Inc.
Baltimore, MD
Dcsigner
Marsha D. Lidard
Neon Knights, Inc.

Red, blue and white neon make up this "patriotic" bike. The 3-ft.-high, 4-ft.-wide bike uses 9mm clear red, blue and 6500 white neon. All of the neon is mounted on a black acrylic backer and encased in a painted wooden shadow box mounted to a wall.

Fabricator
    Kraft Studio
    Washington, DC
Designer
    Craig A. Kraft
    Kraft Studio
Client
    Citibank
Selling price
    $6,800

Fabricated from a positive life-cast, "Fragmented Figure and Light" measures 5 × 5 × 1 ft. The materials used include copper, neon, stained glass and Tecnolux glass.

Fabricator
    Neotericity
    St. Charles, MO
Designer
    Timothy J. Bannick
    Neotericity
Client
    Studio Display
Selling price
    $1,200

Located in a cafe, "Electric Bass" is a neon bass-guitar wall decoration that incorporates 6mm clear and coated ruby tubing with straight argon gas. The neon strings conform to the contours of the mannequin's body. Overall dimensions measure approximately 16 × 48 × 9 in.

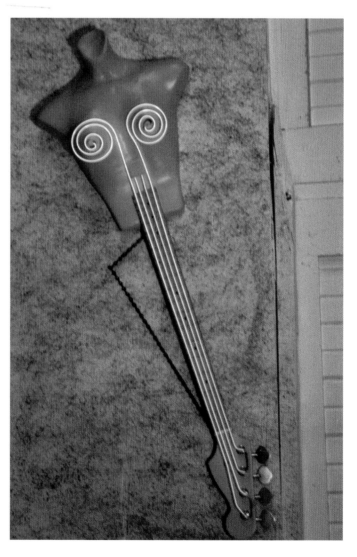

Fabricator
  Kraft Studio
  Washington, DC
Designer
  Craig A. Kraft
  Kraft Studio
Client
  St. Petersburg (Florida) Center for the Arts

For this project, Kraft employs Forton MG acrylic fiberglass for the negative body cast. "Running Man" is lit by neon hidden in channels along the edges of the body cast, which measures 6 ft. tall, 4 ft. wide and 2 ft. deep.

Fabricator
  Kraft Studio
  Washington, DC
Designer
  Craig A. Kraft
  Kraft Studio
Client
  Convergence Art Festival,
  Providence, RI
Selling price
  $22,000

"Falling Man" utilizes Forton MG acrylic fiberglass for the negative body cast. The structure, lit by neon hidden in channels along the edges of the body cast, measures 6 ft. tall, 4 ft. wide and 2 ft. deep.

Fabricator
Superior Sign Systems
Vacaville, CA
Designer
Debra Nichols Design
San Francisco, CA
Account executive
Robert Riddell

Multicolor exposed Tecnolux neon tubing was used for this building decoration. The copy for the 21-in. "Embarcadero Center" and the 36-in. "Cinema" is made of reverse-channel aluminum letters with white-neon halo illumination.

Fabricator
National Sign Corp.
Seattle, WA
Designer
Ken Krumpos
National Sign Corp.
Client
Wings Cafe

The panels for each letter in "Wings" are 18-in.-sq., milled-out, polished stainless steel. The letters are routed out of stainless steel, applied with acrylic and then backlit. Horizon-blue neon provides the halo illumination. "Cafe" is fabricated from cut-out aluminum and has exposed ruby-red neon. Plexiglas® acrylic comprises the airplane graphic and is offset from the background. The sky graphic and image are painted directly onto the wall.

Fabricator
  Neon-Line Werbedesign GmbH
  Vienna, Austria
Designers
  Christine Lindergrün (graphic design)
  Neon-Line Werbedesign GmbH (neon design)

Promoting a salon that styles both men's and women's hair, this sign is enclosed in a customized case that takes the shape of the neon.

Fabricator
  Neon-Line Werbedesign GmbH
  Vienna, Austria
Designers
  Arch. Johannes Kraus and
  Arch. Maria-Rosa Kramer (concept)
  Dusty Sprengnagel and
  Zofia Bialas (neon design)
  Neon-Line Werbedesign GmbH
  Vienna, Austia

Installed in an old tramway hangar converted into an inline skating arena, this 3-D Coke® sign appears to be floating in space. Its red Pyrex® glass for the neon is mounted on adjustable, telescopic tubes, which allowed easy manipulation of the sign during installation. Outside this hangar, a yellow neon tube (mounted on horizontal struts hanging from the ceiling) leads to the main hall. This tube is 25m long. The Coke lettering is 15m long.

Fabricator
Custom Neon Designs, Inc.
Wilmington, DE
Designer
Patricia Pitzer
Illume Creatif
Philadelphia, PA
Client
University of Delaware Trabant Center

For this neon-graphics installation, 81 neon arches are suspended from 30-ft. ceilings and vary in size from 9-12 ft. in radius. The tubes are all in 15mm Voltarc NeoBlue and Clear Gold II. Fabrication involved placing arches and glass tubes in an oven and heating them to form the required radii. More than 480 units of 4-ft. tubes were needed, so steel molds were made by pulling metal angle strips into the radius and welding them onto a frame. The straight glass rods were placed in the cradle of the angle at the top of the "U." Once heated in the oven, the glass pieces conformed to the shape, and were cooled slowly for annealing. They were then cut to size, welded and pumped. End units, zigs and arches were hand-bent.

18-in. aluminum reverse-channel letters. The "V" is a pan-...s® acrylic top for illumination of wall graphics. "Bistro/Bar" is ...t backed with white Plexiglas for internal neon illumination.

Fabricator
National Signs Inc.
Houston, TX
Designer
Javier Garza
National Signs Inc.
Client
Turbo Iwerks/Dave and Buster's
Selling price
$22,000

Several ingredients were needed to create this 5-ft.-wide × 7-ft.-high × 17½-ft.-long restaurant sign. First, the word "Turbo" is channel letters with flexible faces, white neon, white Plexiglas® acrylic and black trim, and "Theater" is routed copy backed with Plexiglas. The sign base is made of .125 aluminum, while the marquee has changeable copy with four lines of 4-in. Wagner dimensional letters. Additionally, various colors of neon are used on the signface. The "Iwerks" sign incorporates white neon, red returns, Plexiglas with red vinyl, a white border and red trim.

Fabricator
Neon-Line Werbedesign GmbH
Vienna, Austria
Designers
Alfred Hager and Dusty Sprengnagel
Neon-Line Werbedesign GmbH

This sign, representing a Vienna night club, measures 180 × 140 cm.

Fabricator
Neon Products
Calgary, AB
Canada
Designers
Richard Emm
Keith Brandt
Neon Products
Client
Flamingo Motel
Selling price
$26,000 (Canadian)

Sheet metal makes up the base of this display, and curved sheet metal forms a semicircle on each of the ends. Rose-colored neon in semicircular shapes is used as an accent. The word "Flamingo" measures 3 × 12 ft. and is a backlit, flat-face sign with painted graphics. "Motel" consists of letters in separate backlit cabinets, each measuring 5 × 2 ft.

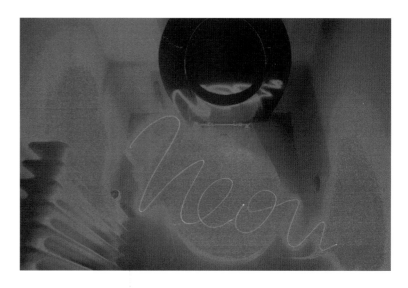

Fabricator
Neon-Line Werbedesign GmbH
Vienna, Austria
Designer
Dusty Sprengnagel
Neon-Line Werbedesign GmbH

This installation — appropriately named "Neon on the Toilet" — consists simply of red tubing bent into the word "neon."

Fabricators
Landmark Sign Co.
Lewisville, TX

National Neon
Duncanville, TX
Designer
Dan Holzschuh
Landmark Sign Co.
Account executive
Dan Holzschuh
Selling price
$5,000

Neon colors that represent computer cable span The Last Byte Cafe, a "breakroom" for Microsoft® employees. According to the fabricators, Microsoft's "think tank" teenagers are asked to relax here for five minutes every hour.

Fabricator
>   Superior Sign Systems
>   Vacaville, CA

Designers
>   Don Brriell and Sayed Aslami
>   Superior Sign Systems

Account executive
>   Earle Gibbings

This 16 × 72-ft. tower sign is fabricated of 16-ft.sq. corrugated aluminum panels with a texcoated finish. The copy is reverse-channel aluminum letters painted to match the tenants' corporate colors. At the bottom of the tower is a concrete base with the city logo; this is embedded into a concrete ground.

Fabricator
>   Walton Signage
>   San Antonio, TX

Designers
>   Antista Design
>   Atlanta, GA
>
>   Sue Johnson
>   Walton Signage

Selling price
> $42,488

This double-faced sign has an internally illuminated pylon. The header and tenant cabinets are routed aluminum with a Plexiglas® acrylic backing; the flags are made of rolled aluminum. The neon, along with translucent vinyl, creates a stripe effect.

Fabricator
Gordon Sign Co.
Denver, CO
Designer
Peter Maggio
Interarc
Denver, CO
Selling price
$20,000

This sign system includes two matching, development marker signs with tenant names. The inner "wedge" is made of Alpolic Stone Series white marble; the lower wedge is Wrisco brushed aluminum. The routed copy is backed by blue Plexiglas® acrylic with T-12 illumination. There are no visible seams or fasteners.

Fabricator
Arrow Sign Co.
Oakland, CA
Designer
Arrow Sign Co.
Account executive
David Staub

The flexible-face K-mart sign in this multi-tenant system is decorated with vinyl. The McDonald's sign, on the other hand, has a flexible-face substrate that's been painted. The overall height of the sign system is 102 ft.

Fabricator
National Sign Corp.
Seattle, WA
Designer
Ken Krumpos
National Sign Corp.
Client
Campus Square
Selling price
$75,000

This 25 × 20-ft. sign has "Campus Square" letters of fabricated aluminum with milled-out centers exposing white neon tucked inside. Horizon-blue neon and halo-blue neon accent the letters. The curved panel acts as a raceway, which also houses a fluorescent lamp with a blue diffuser and a horizon-blue exposed tube that light the panel. The tenant cabinet is fabricated from standard aluminum and features fluorescent illumination.

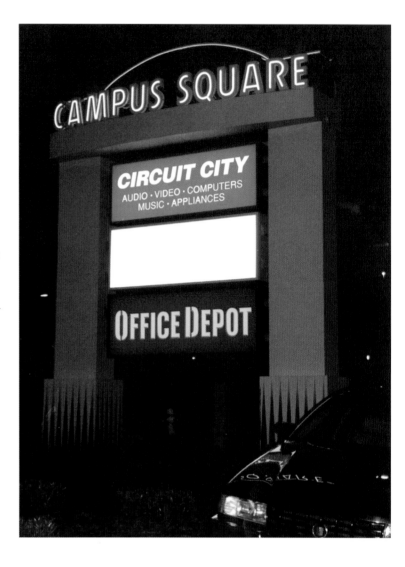

Fabricator
Capital Neon
Sacramento, CA
Designer
Capital Neon
Selling price
$15,800

Measuring 25 ft. high, and with a 12 × 18-ft. double-face, illuminated cabinet, this sign's built to last. "Madison Mall" is painted, routed, textured aluminum, backed with white Plexiglas® acrylic covered by teal, translucent vinyl. The squiggles are exposed yellow neon; the geometric shapes are non-illuminated Gatorfoam™ red squares; and the tenant faces are white Lexan® with red, teal, black and dark-blue vinyl copy.

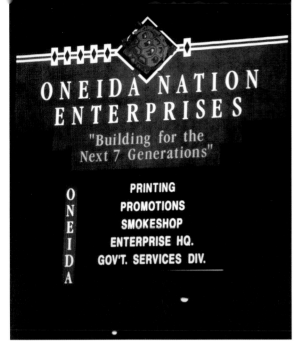

Fabricator
Orde Adv. Inc.
De Pere, WI
Designer
Julie Marohl
Orde Adv. Inc.
Selling price
$10,000

This double-faced, internally illuminated pylon sign has a top cabinet measureing 9 ft. 4 in. × 14 ft. The aluminum tenant cabinet is 5 × 8 ft. and incorporates Lexan® faces with surface-applied, translucent-vinyl copy and graphics.

Fabricator
Capital Neon
Sacramento, CA
Designer
Capital Neon
Selling price
$9,500

This sign has a 15 ft. 2 in. overall height, a cabinet size of 8 × 13 ft., and 24-gauge, textured, sheet-metal construction. The tenant panels have Lexan® faces. The face at the top is routed aluminum with green and red Plexiglas® acrylic. Illumination is via fluorescent lamps.

Fabricator
Sign Productions, Inc.
Cedar Rapids, IA
Designer
Doug Stancel
Marion, IA

A double-face extruded aluminum cabinet with flexible-face fabric is incorporated in this main-ID sign. Opaque background vinyl is employed to give a routed effect at night. The sign is mounted onto a custom brick base.

Fabricator
Sign It
Cornwall, ON
Canada
Designers
Nancy Beaudette
Noella Cotnam
Sign It

Fabricator
US Signs
Houston, TX
Designer
Uri Kelman
Houston, TX

Fabricator
Sign Concepts
Addison, IL
Designer
Al Bolek
Sign Concepts

Fabricator
Tullochgorum Signs
Ormstown, QC
Canada
Designer
Loraine Lamb Lalonde
Tullochgorum Signs

Fabricator
Eric Grohe Design
Marysville, WA
Designer
Eric Grohe
Eric Grohe Design

Fabricator
Carlson Sign Art
Belmont, MI
Designer
Dan Carlson
Carlson Sign Art

Fabricator
David Design
Bryan, OH
Designer
David Showalter
David Design
Client
Victorian Afternoon Teas
Selling price
$700

This 2 × 3-ft., double-sided sign is fabricated from MDO. The text is computer-cut vinyl. The flowers and vines are painted with tinted glaze varnishes; the outlines and borders are hand-painted with lettering enamels.

Fabricator
Tullochgorum Signs
Ormstown, QC
Canada

Designer
Loraine Lamb Lalonde
Tullochgorum Signs

Client
La Bergerie Du Coteau

Selling price
$635 (Canadian)

This 48 × 49-in. farm sign is painted with lettering enamels on ¾-in. simulated wood. It is top-coated, and its edges are sealed with an epoxy. The hand-painted pictorial shows the breed of sheep raised on the farm.

Fabricator
Greg Ross
Summit, NJ
Designer
Greg Ross

Greg Ross built this 4 × 5-ft. sign to advertise his business at different public events. The double-sided sign is hand-painted; the "G.W. Ross" lettering is done in 23K goldleaf.

Fabricator
Custom Art & Signs
DeWitt, IA
Designer
John Steiniger
Custom Art & Signs
Client
Snip & Clip
Selling price
$475

Hand-painted with enamels on ¾-in. MDO, this sign identifies a business offering grooming/rooming services for cats and dogs. The sign measures 6 ft. × 42 in.

Fabricator
> Custom Signs
> Lancaster, ON,
> Canada

Designer
> Louise Macaulay
> Custom Signs

An utterly fantastic cow pictorial, rendered in 1-Shot enamels, graces this 3 × 4-ft., $850, single-sided sign. The sign is made of ¾-in. MDO and features painted finials.

Fabricator
  Sign Design
  Wooster, OH
Designers
  Ken and Stephanie Stiffler
  Sign Design

Fabricated from MDO, this 48 × 92-in. double-sided sign incorporates a background and panel painted with 1-Shot enamel. The sign's graphics and lettering are cut vinyl.

Fabricator
  D&D Signs
  Marysville, CA
Designer
  D&D Signs

Airbrushed pheasant and golfball graphics fit this sign to a tee. These illustrations, rendered with Auto Air paint, are complemented by vinyl graphics coated with Frog Juice. The sign measures 5 × 10 ft.

Fabricator
Sign It
Cornwall, ON
Canada
Designers
Nancy Beaudette
Noella Cotnam
Sign It
Client
Town of Navan

On this 4 × 6-ft., flat, MDO sign, all lettering and graphics are hand-painted.

Fabricator
MCM Graphix
Moundsville, WV
Designers
Matthew and Crista Menard
MCM Graphix

This sign is a gift that keeps on giving. Made of 3 × 4-ft. MDO, it features a painted background, borders and shadows, and an airbrushed banner. The lettering is vinyl.

Fabricator
One Truck Parade
Roswell, NM
Designer
One Truck Parade
Client
Cheyenne Dairy

This dairy sign was hand-painted, roller-blended and lettered.

Fabricator
Shawcraft Sign Co.
Machesney Park, IL
Designers
Jay Allen
Bryan Shattuck
Shawcraft Sign Co.

With its 1-Shot- and Deka-painted backgrounds and vinyl lettering, this sign certainly takes the cake. All panels in the 9 ft. 6-in.-wide, 15 ft. 6-in.-tall sign are 4mm Dibond material, except for the changeable copy board, which is made of Lustreboard, trim cap and red vinyl squares.

The two-piece chef hat is attached to a ½-in. MDO backer and bolted through the sign into 5-in. square steel poles, while the "By the Dozen" panel is spaced 1 in. above the hat.

Interestingly, the sign's brick base — designed to match the building — is actually plastic skirting for mobile homes. This skirting is installed to a frame that is bolted to the metal poles.

Fabricator
Motivational Systems, Inc.
National City, CA
Designer
Marjorie Wakefield
Motivational Systems, Inc.
Account executive
Alan Goya
Client
Pageantry Communities
Selling price
$2,720

These wall-mounted signs are cut from ¾-in.-thick Medex™ material; the lettering is sandblasted and filled with paint. In keeping with the name of the overall project — Monet — the images are reproductions of various Monet paintings. These images were scanned and output as photographic adhesive vinyl, which was then hand-cut to shape. The decorative fasteners used to hang the signs on the wall have a painted finish that looks like copper.

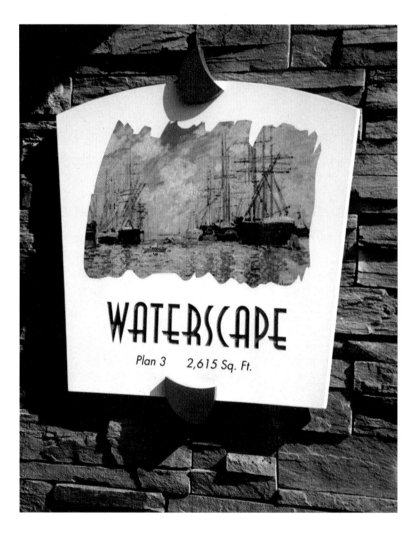

Fabricator
Art Frisbie's Airworx
Lafayette, NJ
Designers
Art Frisbie
Art Frisbie's Airworx

Michael Gawel
Alpine Signs
Sussex, NJ
Client
Spring House Restaurant & Tavern
Selling price
$925

The "S" in "Spring" is cut out and offset from the rest of the lettering to make for a more dynamic sign. The 3 × 8-ft. sign is fabricated from MDO plywood cutouts. The flower on the "S" is a sample of the wallpaper used inside the restaurant; this sample was pasted on aluminum sheeting that was subsequently cut and placed on the sign. The marbleized panel on which the "S" is situated, combined with the goldleaf trim around the sign's border, completes the piece.

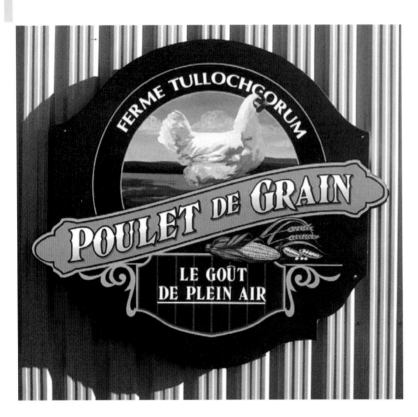

Fabricator
 Tullochgorum Signs
 Ormstown, QC
 Canada
Designer
 Loraine Lamb Lalonde
 Tullochgorum Signs
Client
 Tullochgorum Farm
Selling price
 $750

This ¾-in. simulated-wood sign, featuring chicken, corn, soybean and wheat motifs, was made to promote the farm's grain-fed chicken operation. The majority of the sign is painted with lettering enamels, but the small copy is 2-mil cut vinyl; the blend on the main copy was achieved with the use of a small roller. This sign measures 46 × 48 in., and is mounted on the farm's new storage facility.

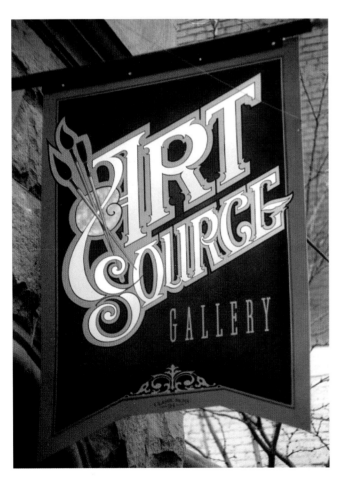

Fabricator
 Classic Design Studio
 Boise, ID
Designers
 Noel Weber
 John McMahon
 Classic Design Studio
Client
 Art Source

This 24 × 48-in. sign is fabricated from aluminum. It has an acrylic urethane finish.

Fabricator
Chuck Kish
Masury, OH
Designer
Chuck Kish
Client
Chestnut St. Cafe

Designed to identify a neighborhood cafe in Masury, OH, this MDO sign attempts to enhance the feeling of dining in small-town USA. Much of the sign is hand-painted. For the scroll work on the edges, however, the fabricator applied masking and then painted it.

Fabricator
Artcraft Signs & Graphics
Pineville, KY
Designer
Russ Mills
Artcraft Signs & Graphics
Client
Renfro's

Made from 5 × 11-ft. MDO, this sign features 23K goldleaf lettering and scrollwork. The background is enamel faux marble, and the banner glazed to achieve a faded pattern. Similarly, the pictorials are designed to further promote an antique look.

Fabricator
  True Identity
  Denver, CO
Designer
  Mark Oatis
  True Identity

A 48 × 120-in. aluminum panel serves as the substrate for this sign. Acrylics are used for the "Mmm mmm good" photo-realistic pictorial; enamels are used for the lettering.

Fabricator
  Vital Signs
  Pensacola, FL
Designer
  Vital Signs

A (wood)work of art, this $500 sign is made of MDO. 1-Shot paint is used for all graphics and lettering.

Fabricator
Matthew Menard
MCM Graphix
Moundsville, WV
Designers
Matthew and Crista Menard
MCM Graphix

Enamel borders and dropshadows are used on this 4 × 6-ft. "pet project." MDO is the substrate-of-choice.

Fabricators
Sign Design
Wooster, OH

Mark Hancock
Bill Walker
Sign Design (installers)

Designers
Ken and Stephanie Stiffler
Sign Design

Fabricated from MDO, this $740, 3 × 8-ft. sign features a background and borders made from 1-Shot lettering enamel. All lettering, shadows, outlines and scrollwork are computer-cut vinyl.

Fabricator
    Vinyl Signs
    Pensacola, FL
Designer
    Vital Signs

Where there's smoke, there's a cigarshop. And at this cigarshop, there's also a $400, 72 × 20-in., painted MDO sign. The ribbon is ⅛-in. Trovicel material, the cigar is Sign Foam®, and the perimeter of the "cigar circle" is gilded. "Grand Reserve" and the small "Cigar & Smoke Shop" are vinyl lettering, while the large "Cigar & Smoke Shop" is painted.

Fabricator
    Sign Concepts
    Addison, IL
Designer
    Al Bolek
    Sign Concepts
Client
    Peaslee Hardware Co.

Mounted on a 6 × 23-ft. board, this ¾-in. MDO sign is flat-painted and airbrushed. It measures 4 × 18 ft.

Fabricator
Island Designs
Captiva, FL
Designers
Chip Carter
Randy Tuthill
Island Designs

Hand-spun gill-ding is used for this fish-restaurant sign. Made of MDO, this $2,200, 36 × 80-in. sign incorporates 1-Shot paint and vinyl graphics.

Fabricator
Vital Signs
Pensacola, FL
Designer
Vital Signs

In addition to its MDO substrate, this $465 sign incorporates computer-cut vinyl lettering, shadows, outlines, scrollwork and graphics. 1-Shot lettering enamel is used for the sign's background, border and vertical stripes.

Fabricators
Faye and Werner Muller
Endless Possibilities
Gananoque, ON
Canada
Designer
Faye Muller
Endless Possibilities

Valued at $2,500, this sign was designed so that its face could be detached and used at tradeshows. Hand-carved wood and formed metal are used for this sign.

Fabricator
Signcraft
Annapolis, MD
Designer
Bill Mackechnie
Signcraft
Client
Katie Bugs
Selling price
$2,200

This double-sided sign measures 4 × 8 ft. × ¾ in. The high-density urethane ladybug has aluminum eyelashes, and the 6 × 6-in. posts are decorated with sandblasted firefly images.

Fabricator
Carlson Sign Art
Belmont, MI
Designer
Karen Johnson
Johnson Design Group
Ada, MI
Client
Johnson Design Group

Among the different materials that make up this sign are a concrete base, a Fiberglas® fabric panel, faux-copper cut-out letters, and mahogany with sandblasted and carved type. The single-faced, freestanding sign measures 40 × 24 × 5 in.

Fabricator
DH Signs of the Times
Victoria, BC
Canada
Designer
DH Signs of the Times
Account executive
Dan Hansen
Client
Page Brook Inc./
Tyndall Wood Devt. Co.
Selling price
$6,500 (Canadian)

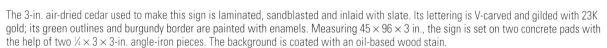

The 3-in. air-dried cedar used to make this sign is laminated, sandblasted and inlaid with slate. Its lettering is V-carved and gilded with 23K gold; its green outlines and burgundy border are painted with enamels. Measuring 45 × 96 × 3 in., the sign is set on two concrete pads with the help of two ¼ × 3 × 3-in. angle-iron pieces. The background is coated with an oil-based wood stain.

Fabricator
Sign It
Cornwall, ON
Canada
Designers
Nancy Beaudette
Noella Cotnam
Sign It
Client
Kinsment Minor Soccer Park

Installed on 6 × 6-in. cedar posts, this sandblasted redwood sign measures 3 × 7 ft. The soccer ball is hand-carved out of 6-in.-thick Sign Foam® high-density urethane.

Fabricator
Boyd Design Group
Englewood, CO
Designer
Boyd Design Group
Client
Iguana's

For this restaurant sign, the lizard was carved out of high-density urethane and applied to a sandblasted Medex™ material background. The curved line below the lettering is gilded with goldleaf; the background is embellished with hammered copper triangles.

Fabricator
  Sign It
  Cornwall, ON
  Canada
Designers
  Nancy Beaudette
  Noella Cotnam
  Sign It
Client
  City of Cornwall

This 4 × 5-ft. park sign is made of sandblasted redwood, and its pictorial is hand-painted with lettering enamels. The sign is installed on 6 × 6-in. posts with 2 × 4-in. cross pieces. A donation plaque is mounted on the back of the sign.

Fabricator
  Bentsen Signs
  E. Greenwich, RI
Designer
  Paul Bentsen
  Bentsen Signs
Client
  Lee Ramond/Marina
Selling price
  $3,500

In this single-sided, 5 × 7-ft. entry sign, the top panel is made of carved, 2-in. balsa. The airbrushed and sandblasted Greenwich Bay image is set against a spatter-painted background. The main sign panel is 2-in., sandblasted redwood — including raised goldleaf letters and redwood framing.

Fabricators
Peter Poanessa
Keene Signworx
Keene, NH

Mary Morse
Chesterfield, NH

A tubular steel frame, MDO panels and a bowl made of 15-lb. Sign Foam® high-density urethane are the ingredients in this saucy, $2,500 sign. Heated and shaped ¼-in. Intecel PVC is used for the fettuccini.

Fabricators
Shawcraft Sign Co.
Machesney Park, IL

Olde Lang Signs (letter routing)
Pittsburgh, PA

Designers
Jay Allen
Joey Marshall
Shawcraft Sign Co.

Nothing but net: This sign features 1 ½-in. Sign Foam® II high-density-urethane letters, painted with 1-Shot enamel and clear coated with Frog Juice. Sandblasted, 1-in.-thick cedar boards — wiped with a lighter color paint to create a "driftwood" appearance — are used on the background panel. Supporting the cedar boards are 2 × 4-in. Southern Yellow Pine pieces bolted to 10-in.-diameter palm tree "trunks."

The splash graphic is made of ¼-in. Lustreboard, with a base coat Deka process-blue paint, airbrushed highlights and a Frog Juice finish. "Island" is painted with 1-Shot, while "Splash Magic" incorporates sunflower-yellow vinyl, a red Krylon fade and a Frog Juice clear coat.

Fabricator
ARTeffects, Inc.
Bloomfield, CT

Designer
Lawrin Rosen
ARTeffects, Inc.

Made for a spring manufacturer, this sign features a clever, dimensional corporate logo on the sign's side. Both the sign itself and the lettering comprise .125-in., fabricated aluminum. The sign measures approximately 6 ft. tall, 15 ft. long and 4 ft. deep.

Fabricator
US Signs
Houston, TX
Designer
Uri Kelman
Houston, TX

Appropriately reflecting the somber tone of this museum, this simple, understated 8 × 10-ft. sign is fabricated aluminum with white dimensional copy. Mirror-polished stainless steel is used for the "shawl and flame"; the flames twirl around each other, while tapering to a point on both axes. All metal and masonry work were donated for this $9,936 sign.

Fabricator
True Identity
Denver, CO
Designer
Mark Oatis
True Identity

This 5 ft. 6 in. × 3-ft. sales information sign for a new home community is made with 1-in.-thick 15-lb. Sign Foam® laminated to 1-in. MDO. The face of the sign is sandblasted, hand-carved and roughed with stones to achieve a fossilized effect. The sandblasted graphics are infilled with paint, and the background is painted with a faux finish to resemble an ancient stone tablet. The painted posts are 4-ft. round peeler logs further enhanced with routed lines, wood caps and bases to represent columns.

Fabricator
Keene Signworx
Keene, NH
Designer
Peter Poanessa
Keene Signworx

A "Keene" sense of design and layout, combined with clear-heart redwood — pre-finished, then carved on a CNC router table — give this sign its style. The "Keene" lettering is cut-out, raised and prism-cut applique.

icator
land Designs
aptiva, FL
gner
hip Carter
land Designs

el Steakhouse's 42 × 68-in. sign is well-done, indeed. Made with Sign Foam® high-density urethane, 3,000 sign was sandblasted using a Grain Fraim grain-making device. Golden Era Studios clip-art is for the border details, and Duracaps are used for the finials. The center of the "S" is faux-marble; her lettering incorporates engine-turned SignGold film.

Fabricator
Sign Classics
New Paltz, NY
Designer
Brian Kurzius
Sign Classics
Client
Lady Tremaine Clothing Store
Selling price
$2,700

This 2 × 10-ft. MDO wall sign has an imitation-marble painted background and raised letters gilded with 23K goldleaf. The raised, carved, cameo design is reproduced century cameo.

Fabricator
Custom Craftsman Signs
Sevierville, TN
Designer
Brother Zank
Custom Craftsman Signs

Time is money — $8,000 worth, to be exact. This 6-ft. carved and blasted sign features 3¾-in.-thick, layered Sign Foam® high-density uretha around a steel support frame. All digits, scrolls and inlines are carved and gilded; the clock letters are applied PVC. Replaceable, fabric tasse hang from a hand-forged iron scroll on the end of the sign.

Fabricator
David Design
Bryan, OH
Designers
David Showalter
David Design

Gary Anderson
Bloomington Design
Bloomington, IN

This 3 × 4-ft. single-faced sign is composed of sand-blasted redwood. The letters are cut-out urethane foam with beveled edges. The sign is hand-tooled and gilded with 24K gold. Finish paint is latex acrylic.

Fabricator
Classic Design Studio
Boise, ID
Designers
Mike Murie
Bryce Twitchell
Classic Design Studio
Client
Murie Design Group

This 24-in. circular wall sign is fabricated from MDF with an acrylic urethane finish. The pencil is hand-carved with Sign Foam® and cast from urethane.

Fabricator
Sign It
Cornwall, ON
Canada
Designers
Nancy Beaudette
Noella Cotnam
Sign It
Client
Farm Boy Food Market

This 9 × 32-ft. single-faced wall sign includes a hand-carved logo composed of laminated Sign Foam® high-density urethane mounted on a sandblasted redwood panel. The carved, prismatic letters have a hand-painted fade, and the background is black smalt.

Fabricator
Carlson Sign Art
Belmont, MI
Designer
Dan Carlson
Carlson Sign Art
Client
The Rhino Pit Bar & Grill

The 40 × 50-in. wall sign incorporates a sandblasted and carved redwood panel with carved Sign Foam® artwork and 23K gold lettering with a blended enamel finish.

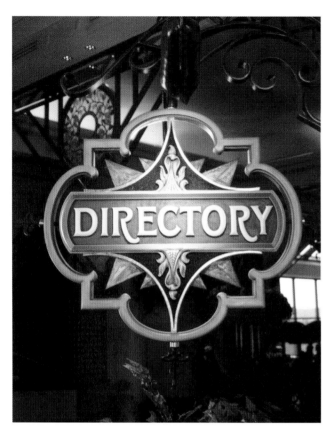

Fabricator
Bentsen Signs
East Greenwich, RI
Designer
Paul Bentsen
Bentsen Signs
Client
Foxwoods Resort-Casino
Selling price
$3,400

This 28 × 30-in. directory sign has an outer frame composed of 2-in. Sign Foam® high-density urethane. The panel is carved and sand-texture painted. Soldered copper triangle points, black glass smalt panels and relief-carved leaf designs accent the copy.

Fabricator
Jon and Karen Ritchey
Pueblo, CO
Designers
Jon Ritchey
John Mendoza
Client
The Latino Chamber of
Commerce of Pueblo
Selling price
$9,600

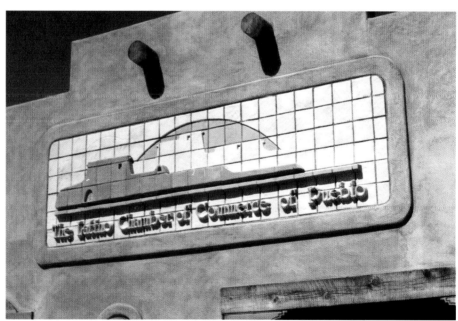

This 4 × 14-ft. wall sign is composed of sculpted and glazed tile units with raised relief.

Fabricator
  True Identity
  Denver, CO
Designers
  Mark Oatis
  True Identity

  Bill Hueg (pictorial)
  Denver, CO

Were she painted on canvas, you'd expect to find "Rosalita" hanging above a mantle, or perhaps, in a museum. Yet this lifelike rendering — designed by Bill Hueg — makes its home on a sign in Sunset Station Hotel & Casino. In addition to its pictorial, the 48 × 58-in. MDF sign features carved and gilded Sign Foam® high-density urethane and compo roses.

Fabricator
  True Identity
  Denver, CO
Designer
  Mark Oatis
  True Identity

Rolled and hand-cut ⅛-in. aluminum and Gerber-router-cut and hand-finished Sign Foam® high-density urethane are used in this 120 × 48-in. sign. So too are trompe l'oeil scrolls and copperleaf.

Fabricator
  True Identity
  Denver, CO
Designers
  David Butler
  Syracuse, IN

  Dan King (Bracket)
  True Identity

With its Gerber-router-cut hand-finished scrolls, hand-painted pictorials and hand-hammered steel bracket, this sign certainly deserves an "Ole!" The 42-in.-diameter sign is made of MDF material.

Fabricator
True Identity
Denver, CO
Designers
Mark Oatis
True Identity

David Butler (lettering)
Syracuse, IN

Gilded, hand-carved, Sign Foam® lettering gives this 67 × 39-in. display its sign-shine. A background made of stained glass and acrylic leading contributes to the sign's unique appearance, as does an ornate, faux-copper-patina border of carved MDF and Sign Foam.

Fabricators
Lynn and Jeremiah Wilkerson
Great Big Signs, Inc.
Kyle, TX

Mario Munoz
Kyle, TX
Designers
Lynn and Timothy Wilkerson
Great Big Signs, Inc.

A sign with "reel" appeal, this $24,000 display is sculpted from EPS foam and incorporates a sanded foam coat over an angle-iron welded framework. The 1-ft.-thick, convex letters in "Cinema 4" are also sculpted EPS, as are the 4 × 52-ft. filmstrip façade and 12-ft.-diameter film reel. 1-Shot enamels — used for the sign's "big finish" — earn the creation an enthusiastic "two thumbs up."

Fabricator
 ARTeffects, Inc.
 Bloomfield, CT
Designer
 Sonolysts
 Waterford, CT

A 6 × 3-ft. blade sign, this display uses cut acrylic sprayed with lacquer. The turtle is made from Sign Foam® high-density urethane and painted with enamels.

Fabricator
 Northport WoodSmiths
 Northport, NY
Designer
 Lee Holcomb
 Northport WoodSmiths

Designed in CorelDraw!, this 10 × 6-ft., $7,200 sign features an MDF figure cut out on an AXYZ router and faux-finished. The background around "Industrial" is v-grooved; peaks of the texture were lightly rollered with red paint, creating a neonlike, edge-light effect.

 Faux goldleaf and a bright yellow border are used on the lettering. "Art" is router-cut from ¾-in. MDO, and is pinned off the surface 2 in. to accentuate the letters' white edging. "Sculpture" is carved in the gray "concrete" border.

 All paint used on the sign is water-based Deka acrylic. Also, at the client's request, the entire sign is made of recycled or reclaimed materials.

Fabricator
    Carlson Sign Art
    Belmont, MI
Designer
    Penny Jane
    Carlson Sign Art
Client
    One Trick Pony Restaurant & Bar
Selling price
    $2,000

This 60 × 90-in. double-faced sign is fabricated from sandblasted cedar with a Sign Foam® high-density urethane lettering logo and borders. The sign includes 23K gold letters and accents.

Fabricator
    Sign It
    Cornwall, ON
    Canada
Designers
    Nancy Beaudette
    Noella Cotnam
    Sign It
Client
    Gumbolini's Restaurant

The oval-shaped wall sign is composed of a 3 × 6-ft. sandblasted redwood panel with prismatic carved letters gilded with 23K gold. Letters, crab and oysters are carved and painted Sign Foam® high-density urethane.

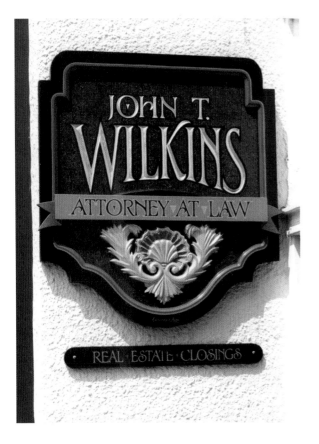

Fabricator
Sign Classics
New Paltz, NY
Designer
Brian Kurzius
Sign Classics
Client
John Wilkins, Attorney at Law
Selling price
$1,800

This 3 × 4-ft. wall sign lettering is carved from Sign Foam® high-density urethane with an imitation granite background. The lower ornamental design is goldleafed.

Fabricators
Keene Signworx
Keene, NH

Mark Goodnough
Keene, NH
Designers
Peter Poanessa
Keene Signworx

Yasvin Design
Hancock, NH

Melded steel — ground and sprayed with emron — is used for the large, gray portion of this sign. The raised black section is ½-in. PVC. But it's the hammered-copper coffee beans that really give this $2,500 sign its flavor.

Fabricator
Classic Design Studio
Boise, ID
Designers
Noel Weber
Jennifer O'Reilly
Classic Design Studio
Client
Zeppole Bakery

This 2 × 4-ft. window sign incorporates multiple shades of variegated and composition goldleaf. Asphaltum shading and mother-of-pearl accents are used on a red marble background with a parchment effect behind the lettering.

Fabricator
Solar Graphics, Inc.
St. Petersburg, FL
Designer
Solar Graphics, Inc.
Client
Art Department
Selling price
$700

This 5 × 7-ft. transparent reflective display features a "negative space" technique that allows the background to show through the design, outlining the image.

Fabricator
  Solar Graphics, Inc.
  St. Petersburg, FL
Designer
  Craig Klafeta
  Solar Graphics, Inc.
Client
  Musicana Dinner Theater
Selling price
  $3,600

The 12 × 35-ft. display incorporates opaque-black and translucent-white films. Low-wattage backlighting makes the white areas glow at night.

Fabricator
  Classic Design Studio
  Boise, ID
Designer
  Noel Weber
  John McMahon
  Dennis Chase
  Classic Design Studio
Client
  Grape Escape Wine Shop

This 2½ × 6-ft. sign is composed of goldleaf on glass, screen-printed halftone backed with gold, prismatic letters and faux stone to match the merchant's floor.

Fabricator
Festival Sign Service
Gainesville, FL
Designer
Robert Rucker
Festival Sign Service
Client
Chesnut's Office and
Art Outfitters
Selling price
$750

This window sign is rendered on a 3 × 6-ft. pane with 23K goldleaf copy and border. Copy outlines and drop shadows are burgundy.

Fabricator
California Signs & Designs
Oceanside, CA
Designer
Steve Davidson
California Signs & Designs
Client
Bear Lake Pizza Co.
Selling price
$1,600

This sign is composed of goldleaf, glass, mother-of-pearl, abalone and 1-Shot paint. The lettering is gilded on glue-chipped glass.

Fabricator
Sign Design
Wooster, OH
Designers
Ken and Stephanie Stiffler
Sign Design

Computer-cut vinyl letters and "sponged" highlights make up this 3 × 4-ft. window graphic. The selling price is $185.

Fabricator
Al Bolek
Sign Concepts
Addison, IL
Designers
Al and Lynda Bolek
Sign Concepts

The 2 × 4-ft. graphic for this hair salon is painted with lettering enamels.

Fabricator
MCM Graphix
Moundsville, WV
Designer
Matthew Menard
MCM Graphix

This 3 × 5-ft. graphic, featuring HP vinyl letters, is painted in reverse. For the airbrushed frame, MCM Graphix used metallic-silver and black enamel paints. The "marbling" is created with silver, white and black enamels. The cost of the graphic is $450.

Fabricator
Shawcraft Sign Co.
Machesney Park, IL
Designer
Jay Allen
Shawcraft Sign Co.

This sign incorporates black vinyl-letter outlines with SignGold 22 vinyl fill. A Universal Products "True Shadow" vinyl is used for the drop-shadow. Notice that the background is sponge-painted using three colors between the dark-green outlines of the "wagon wheel." In addition, the border is airbrushed with a beveled edge, and the entire background is rolled with a lighter mint green. The entire sign is painted in reverse.

Fabricator
MCM Graphix
Moundsville, WV
Designer
Matthew Menard
MCM Graphix

For this graphic, which is painted in reverse, MCM Graphix used enamel paints. Notice the "roller-blended" letters, as well as the etched-glass vinyl stripes. The graphic sells for $175.

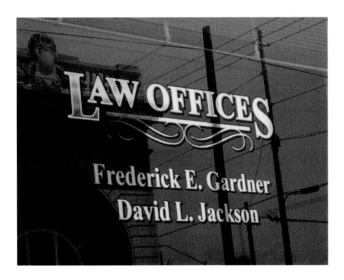

Fabricators
Matthew and Crista Menard
MCM Graphix
Moundsville, WV
Designer
Matthew Menard
MCM Graphix

This sign is decorated with 22K goldleaf with signgold burnished centers and hand-gilded matte outlines. The lettering is outlined in black and drop-shadowed. The sign sells for $800.

Fabricator
Eric Grohe Design
Marysville, WA
Designer
Eric Grohe
Eric Grohe Design
Client
Royal Estate Corp.Cornerstone Square
Ohio Bureau of Employment Services

As part of the renovation of a structure erected in 1920, two sides of the building, encompassing an area of 14,000 sq. ft., were resurfaced with Drivit® insulated architectural finish. This artificial surface was designed to match the brick and terra cotta details of the other two sides of the building. The entire replacement surface was then painted to resemble these original materials.

Fabricator
Eric Grohe Design
Marysville, WA
Designer
Eric Grohe
Eric Grohe Design
Client
American Hop Museum and
Toppenish Mural Society

These 18 × 42-ft. and 18 × 90-ft. painted murals depict the various stages of the hop production and brewing process. The murals are oil-painted on a prepared masonry surface.

Fabricator
Eric Grohe Design
Marysville, WA
Designer
Eric Grohe
Eric Grohe Design
Client
City of Port Orchard, WA

This 14 × 71-ft. Centennial Mural is painted on the side of the public library building. Sculptural relief paintings are placed below the windows; the color murals are painted using photographs of human models posed in period costumes.

Fabricator
Eric Grohe Design
Marysville, WA
Designer
Eric Grohe
Eric Grohe Design
Client
City of Steubenville, OH

The City of Steubenville commissioned this mural depicting the steel production process that is the backbone of the local economy. Working from a scale drawing, the designer drafted the main image and architecture on the wall. Acrylic paint was used on prepared masonry.

Fabricator
Eric Grohe Design
Marysville, WA
Designer
Eric Grohe
Eric Grohe Design
Client
City of Steubenville, OH

This Centennial Arch mural measures 28 ft. 6 in × 97 ft. 6 in. It is painted on the side of a brick building that was resurfaced with Drivit® architectural finish. The architecture and scenery are drafted freehand. The image is based on early photographs of the town.

Fabricator
Signworks
Torquay, S.Devon
England
Designer
David Smith
Signworks
Client
Carousel Cookery

This 2 × 8-ft., hand-painted, airbrushed plywood sign also employs some cut-vinyl graphics.

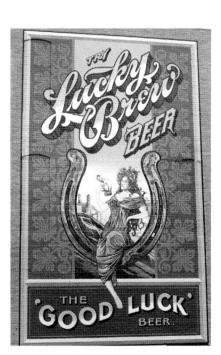

Fabricator
True Identity
Denver, CO
Designer
Mark Oatis
True Identity

For this casino's 19 × 33-ft. graphic, True Identity uses enamels on exterior brick.

Fabricator
    Eric Grohe Design
    Marysville, WA
Designer
    Eric Grohe
    Eric Grohe Design

This 46 × 38-ft. mural was commissioned to honor the high-school football tradition in Massillon, OH. Every element of the wall, including the ivy, is painted. Eric Grohe uses Sherwin Williams Super Paint and Triangle Coatings, Inc.'s Trilon™ overcoat.

Fabricator
    Eric Grohe Design
    Marysville, WA
Designer
    Eric Grohe
    Eric Grohe Design

For this project, Eric Grohe first power-washes the brick wall. Then, only to those areas that would receive paint, he applies a coating of Loxon by Sherwin Williams. The mural is painted using Sherwin Williams Super Paint; it's overcoated with Triangle Coatings, Inc's Trilon™. To transfer the image onto the wall, Grohe works from a small-scaled drawing and uses a tape measure and chalk line to determine the image area. Finally, the boat and the girl and boy are photographed with slide film, projected onto the wall at night, and then filled with paint.

Fabricator
Eric Grohe Design
Marysville, WA
Designer
Eric Grohe
Eric Grohe Design

Originally, this five-story parking garage was made of gray, cast-in-place concrete. All the visible exterior surfaces are painted to represent "real" materials. The surface contains an application of Keim Grob as well as Keim Concrete paint. Using laser and hand-cut stencils, the Keim Mineral paint is applied to the surface (primarily by hand). An airless sprayer is used to apply the brick pattern.

Fabricator
Eric Grohe Design
Marysville, WA
Designer
Eric Grohe
Eric Grohe Design

This one-point-perspective mural adorns the entrance of a New York shopping mall. Architectural elements common to the facade are used to frame a scene of the falls. The people in the mural are actual mall visitors. Eric Grohe transferred their photographs to the wall by pouncing the outline of their images and then detailing them with paint. The mural was painted using Pittsburgh Sun Proof exterior latex and then overcoated with ABR-404 Graffiti Stop by ABR Products, Inc.

Fabricator
Eric Grohe Design
Marysville, WA
Designer
Eric Grohe
Eric Grohe Design

The sculptural elements on either side of this 34 × 34-ft. wall mural depicts the City of Steubenville's domestic and industrial development. The wall is made of Drivit® surfacing material; the wall's artwork incorporates Sherwin Williams Super Paint and an overcoat of ABR-404 Graffiti Stop.

Fabricator
  Bert Graphix
  Pompton Lakes, NJ
Designer
  Albert Quimby
  Bert Graphix
Client
  Gary Wright

The lettering for this project is airbrushed, and the window glass is made with a varnish shade to appear tinted.

Fabricator
Bert Graphix
Pompton Lakes, NJ
Designer
Albert Quimby
Bert Graphix
Client
DT Allen Contracting

This vehicle graphic features a hand-painted tractor with varnish shading, a granite stone panel and an airbrushed lettering inline/outline.

Fabricator
Bert Graphix
Pompton Lakes, NJ
Designer
Albert Quimby
Bert Graphix
Client
Treasure Coast Auto Transport

Goldleaf lettering with a varnish shade is used on this vehicle. An airbrushed background with a custom-painted roadster complete the graphic.

Fabricator
Reid Signs
Seattle, WA
Designer
Greg Reid
Reid Signs
Client
Able Pest Control
Selling price
$1,000

For this sign, Able Pest Control's logo was completely redesigned. In the new version, a graphic of a dead rat is used as part of the letter "A" in Able. The red oval includes a tiled pattern of ants and moths, and a loose script style is used for the lettering. Plus, the entire vehicle is pinstriped.

Fabricator
Bert Graphix
Pompton Lakes, NJ
Designer
Albert Quimby
Bert Graphix
Client
Kodiak Landscape Design

The picture of the bear is hand-painted. The lettering is airbrushed inline/outline.

Fabricator
Bert Graphix
Pompton Lakes, NJ
Designer
Albert Quimby
Bert Graphix
Client
Criaer Auto Body

The lettering is airbrushed and shaded with varnish. The oval is painted to give a diamond-plate look.

Fabricator
Imaginality, Inc.
Minneapolis, MN
Designer
Francis Lu
Imaginality, Inc.
Account Executive
Myrna Orensten
Client
Breadsmith
Selling price
$1,300

Five different colors of vinyl are used to create these graphics.

Fabricator
Bert Graphix
Pompton Lakes, NJ
Designer
Albert Quimby
Bert Graphix

This vehicle-identification graphic is hand-painted and airbrushed; "Paving" is rendered in goldleaf. The Mack-Truck cartoon is customized.

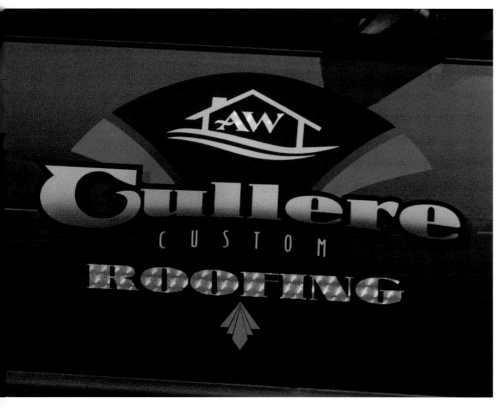

Fabricator
Bert Graphix
Pompton Lakes, NJ
Designer
Albert Quimby
Bert Graphix

Here, Bert Graphix, Pompton Lakes, NJ, airbrushes the company name, "Cullere." Silver leaf is used for the word "Roofing."

Fabricator
Bert Graphix
Pompton Lakes, NJ

Designer
Albert Quimby
Bert Graphix

This entirely hand-painted graphic incorporates gold leaf and a picture of a Corvette.

Fabricator
Bert Graphix
Pompton Lakes, NJ

Designer
Albert Quimby
Bert Graphix

Hand-painting and airbrushing are used to create this "eagle" graphic; the "star" is gilded.

Fabricator
Bert Graphix
Pompton Lakes, NJ

Designer
Albert Quimby
Bert Graphix

This graphic is hand-painted and airbrushed; "Criger" is shaded using varnish.

Fabricator
Bert Graphix
Pompton Lakes, NJ
Designer
Albert Quimby
Bert Graphix

Gold leaf, a carbon-fiber panel, an airbrush-faded paint job, vinyl and varnish shades accent this vehicle graphic.

Fabricator
Michael Paul
Auto Graphix
Kinnelon, NJ
Designer
Michael Paul
Auto Graphix

Hand-painted and airbrushed with marble effect, this sign is fabricated using enamel-receptive high-performance vinyl.
It was transferred on site.

Fabricator
Bert Graphix
Pompton Lakes, NJ
Designer
Albert Quimby
Bert Graphix
Client
R&D Septic Service

This truck displays a hand-painted cartoon and airbrushed lettering.

Fabricator
Bert Graphix
Pompton Lakes, NJ
Designer
Albert Quimby
Bert Graphix
Client
Green Meadow Landscaping

In this sign, the pictorial is painted and airbrushed by hand. The lettering is varnish-shaded.

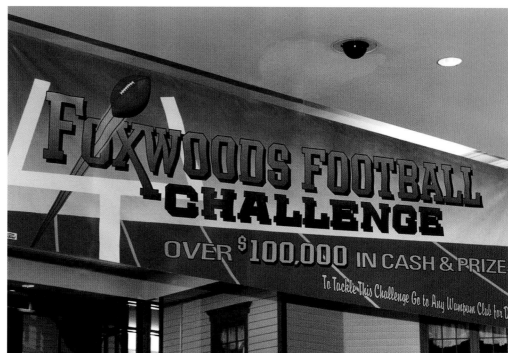

Fabricator
  ARTeffects, Inc.
  Bloomfield, CT
Designers
  Lawrin Rosen
  Robert Fisher
  ARTeffects, Inc.
Account executive
  Lawrin Rosen
Client
  Foxwoods Casino
Selling price
  $395

This 20-ft.-long banner features airbrushed computer-cut vinyl graphics.

Fabricator
 Tramps Designs
 Mississauga, ON
 Canada
Designer
 Tramp Warner
 Tramps Designs
Client
 1-Shot/Denver Letterheads

Decorated with 1-Shot paints, the US Banner material is paneled, roller-painted, and air-brush-trimmed.

Fabricator
Tramps Designs
Mississauga, ON
Canada
Designer
Tramp Warner
Tramps Designs
Client
Letterheads, Fargo, SD

This US Banner material is painted with all 1-Shot products. The small lettering is masked and roller-painted.

Fabricator
Tramps Designs
Mississauga, ON
Canada
Designer
Tramp Warner
Tramps Designs
Client
Eastern States Sign Council (ESSC)

US Banner material is used to create this sign. Hand-lettering, airbrushing and vinyl application are among the fabrication techniques employed.

Fabricator
Sign Concepts
Addison, IL
Designers
Al and Lynda Bolek
Sign Concepts

Sign Concepts created this banner for Giovanni's restaurant. It measures 3 × 5 ft. and incorporates paint and vinyl.

Fabricator
Colorburst Signs
and Graphics
Denver, CO
Designer
Marty Hammond
Denver, CO
Client
Denver Zoo
Selling price
$1,900

This double-faced, 16-oz. vinyl banner is screen printed. A total of 16 such banners were made, each measuring 3 × 8 ft.

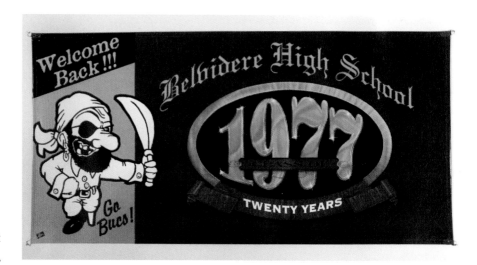

Fabricator
Shawcraft Sign Co.
Machesney Park, IL
Designer
Jay Allen
Shawcraft Sign Co.

This 3 × 6-ft. Regal banner incorporates 1-Shot paint with Spar-Cal vinyl used in other areas. SignGold 22 is added to the letters "Class of," and the numbers are beveled and airbrushed for a brassy look.

Fabricator
Sign Concepts
Addison, IL
Designer
Al and Lynda Bolek
Sign Concepts

This 2 × 6-ft. Signtex banner, designed in Signlab 4.95, incorporates vinyl and paint.

Fabricator
MCM Graphix
Moundsville, WV
Designer
Matthew Menard
MCM Graphix

This $170 banner was designed for Wildscape, Inc., a hand-crafted jewelry shop. Measuring 2 × 6 ft., the banner features vinyl letters with airbrushed dropshadows and highlights. The pictorial was printed using Roland's ColorCAMM.

Fabricator
Signs, Inc.
Honolulu, HI
Designer
Dave Kembel
Bishop Museum
Honolulu, HI

Signs, Inc. fabricated these banners for the Kaho'olawe exhibit at the Bishop Museum in Honolulu, HI. The banners feature vinyl on vinyl; four banners with the same design were made for the museum, and ranged in price from $390 to $1485.

Fabricator
Sign Concepts
Addison, IL
Designer
Al and Lynda Bolek
Sign Concepts

Paint and vinyl were used to create this colorful 3 × 15-ft. Signtex banner.

Fabricator
Classic Design Studio
Boise, ID
Designers
Lisa Pisano
Old Boise Guitar Co.
Boise, ID

Noel Weber
John McMahon
Classic Design Studio
Client
Old Boise Guitar Co.

Sandblasted and decorated with gold-leaf, this glass sign measures 32 × 60 in. The guitar is set against a faux-marble background.

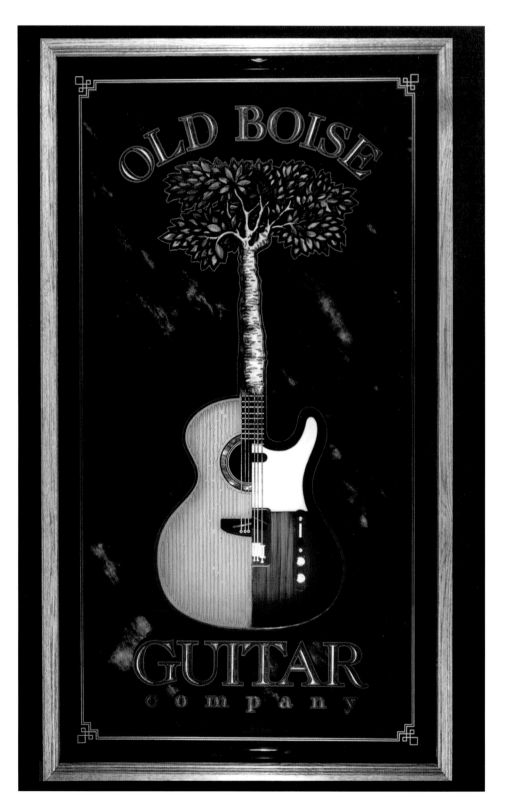

Fabricator
Classic Design Studio
Boise, ID
Designer
Noel Weber
Classic Design Studio
Client
Bruce Willis

This 12 × 48-in., glue-chipped, silvered sign has goldleaf lettering.

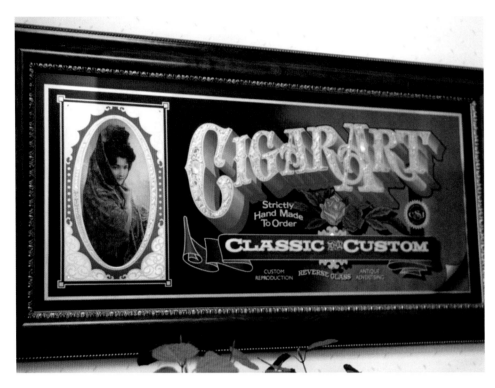

Fabricator
LA Signs and Graphics
Los Angeles, CA
Designer
John Studden
LA Signs and Graphics
Client
Cigar Art
Selling price
$2,500

This 42 × 22-in. glass sign is reverse-painted, blended and glue-chipped. It incorporates 23 and 18K gold, a pictorial, abalone shell, 1-Shot paint and a stippled background.

Fabricators
Grand Illusions, Inc.
Apopka, FL

Sunbelt Metals and Mfg., Inc.
Apopka, FL
Designers
Tom Yorke
WDI Creative
WDIFL Magic Kingdom
Lake Buena Vista, FL

Larry Fann
Ken Westerman
Dave Fann, Grand Illusions, Inc.
Account executive
Larry Fann, Grand Illusions, Inc.
Client
Walt Disney World
Crystal Palace Marquee
Selling price
$23,000

The marquee measures 4½ × 9½ ft. with a ½-in.-thick plate glass cut to pattern shape. The background is sandblasted and glue-chipped. The logo and lettering are hand-painted and airbrushed with enamel paints. Goldleaf areas include Schwabacher premium 16.7K pale gold and Swift 23K deep goldleaf. The sign's entire back is painted for protection.

Fabricator
California Signs & Designs
Oceanside, CA
Designer
Steve Davidson
California Signs & Designs
Client
Wells Optometry

All lettering is 23K goldleaf. "Dr. Melinda Wells" is matte gold; the glasses and "Wells" are matte with outline. "Quality Eyecare, Quality Eyewear" lettering is vinyl, with the background done in a sponge effect that matches the client's countertop. The lighter color makes it appear as if there is glass in the glasses.

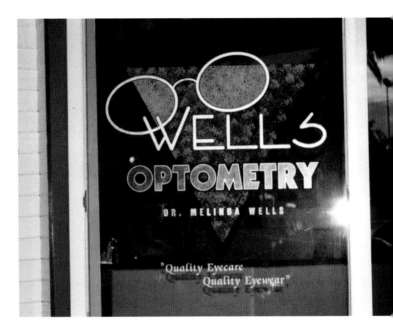

Fabricator
Classic Design Studio
Boise, ID
Designer
Noel Weber
Classic Design Studio

This 16 × 48-in. sandblasted sign includes goldleaf.

Fabricator
  True Identity
  Denver, CO
Designer
  Mark Oatis
  True Identity

This 24 × 108-in. sign features glue chipping, abalone inlays, watch crystals, double-split shades, gold leaf, copper leaf, blended paint fields, carved scrolls and plaid burnish.

Fabricator
  True Identity
  Denver, CO
Designer
  Mark Oatis
  True Identity

True Identity got the bid to do this glass sign for the Station Casino in Kansas City, KS. Measuring 4 ft. high × 17 ft., 4 in. long, the sign incorporates stage blasting, glue chipping, abalone inlays, watch crystals, dimensional burnish, split-blended shades, cast-resin oak leaves and beveled glass.

Fabricator
Karman Ltd.
Canega Park, CA
Designer
Wieber Nelson Design
San Diego, CA

This $145,000 sign was created for the University of California, San Diego Medical Center. The sign features a front and back layer of ¼-in. tempered glass with a core panel of ½-in. acrylic. Both layers of glass are sandblasted and filled in with three airbrushed colors. The primary signs range in size from 36 × 18 in. to 36 × 48 in.

Fabricator
LA Signs and Graphics
Los Angeles, CA
Designer
John Studden
LA Signs and Graphics

Central Cigar commissioned LA Signs and Graphics to create this gilded-glass, reverse-screened sign. Measuring 42 in. wide, it contains a pictorial, which is reverse-painted, blended and airbrushed, and is placed in an abalone oak frame.

Fabricator
LA Signs and Graphics
Los Angeles, CA
Designer
John Studden
LA Signs and Graphics

To create this oval-shaped, 48 × 36-in. glass sign, LA Signs and Graphics mixed glue chipping, gilding, drop shadows, abalone wings and body-trans enamel, watch crystal eyes and airbrushing. The frame is made from carved mahogany.

Fabricator
> Cleveland Metroparks
> Graphics Div.
> Brecksville, OH

Designer
> Cleveland Metroparks
> Graphics Div.

Client
> Emerald Necklace Marina

Mates at the Emerald Necklace Marina are sure to enjoy this swashbuckling sign system; it's a veritable nautical nirvana.

The 12 × 5-ft. facility sign, for example, has two separate, sandblasted cedar boards. The back board was edge-routed before sandblasting, then stained gray. And on the oval sign board, the lettering and borders were masked, and the background was blasted away. Hand-sanding was used to give the borders their rounded shape. Then, the background was stained, the borders painted and the letters goldleafed. Sintra® material was airbrushed to create the boat background; the ship was screen printed. With these elements assembled, a rope trip was placed around the oval sign, and the lights installed.

In the marina's main hall hang the 24 × 18-in. Sails Point and restroom signs. These sandblasted cedar signs are used to indicate specific areas of the marina and are finished much like the facility sign. Their aluminum brackets are fabricated and painted to match the goldleaf.

At the end of the hall that houses the Sails Point and restroom signs is the entrance to the Waterside Room. The 6-ft. × 30-in. sign for this room features an anchor, styled after one used in a Lake Erie commercial sailing vessel. In addition, the sign includes carved and sandblasted cedar, fabricated to simulate a ribbon from the fan tail of the aforementioned Lake Erie ship. The 30-in.-tall stanchion is placed in front of the doors to keep the public from disturbing an event in progress. It is constructed of sandblasted cedar posts and assembled with rope and an accompanying sign.

Fabricator
Western Signs
Diamond Springs, CA
Designers
Michael Dunlavey
Sacramento, CA

Yvonne Guerra
Sacramento, CA
Client
El Dorado Hills Devt. Co./
Serrano El Dorado
Selling price
$150,000

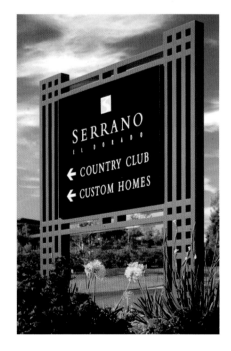

"Grid" is the word when it comes to signage at the Serrano El Dorado development. Fabricated with 1-3-in. steel tubing, each piece of the grid-like structures is cut to size, welded into place and grinded down for a molded finish look. The sign faces themselves are interchangeable aluminum pans with concealed fasteners, and feature a color scheme of deep green, metallic black and copperleaf. Sign sizes range from 51 ft. wide × 49 ft. high to 5½ ft. wide × 12 ft. high.

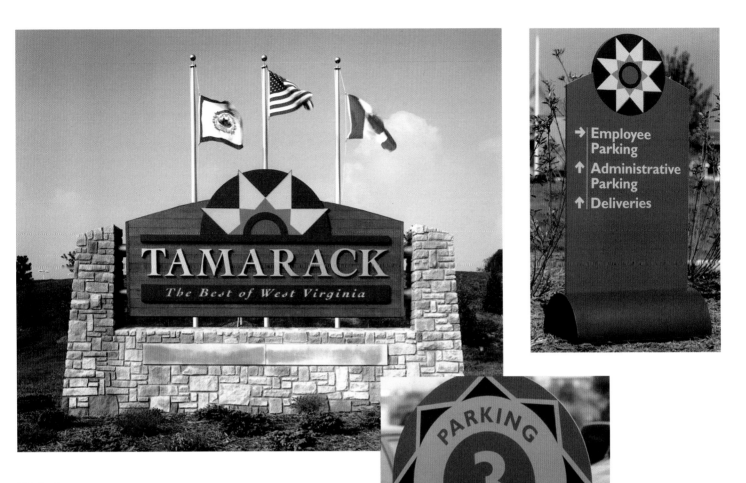

Fabricator
 Paris Signs
 Lavalette, WV
Designer
 Susan Hessler
 Columbus, OH
Client
 Tamarack Cultural Arts Center

Located in West Virginia, the Tamarack Cultural Arts Center is a unique facility that showcases a statewide collection of handmade crafts, arts and cuisine. Throughout the center's exterior signage program, symbol elements are used; these mimic traditional quilt patterns, as well as the facility's pointed architectural design. A vibrant color palette reflects colors found in the West Virginia landscape.

 The sign system includes a main entrance/identity sign, as well as informational signage that identifies Artisan Studios and handicap parking. To make the program cost effective and to facilitate fabrication and installation, existing metal extrusions were used for the directional pylon bases, and existing metal tubing and brackets were used for all pole signs. Directional pylon sign panels are made of Komacel material with routed graphics on top. Graphics and lettering are made of vinyl.

Fabricator
ARTeffects, Inc.
Bloomfield, CT
Designer
Amenta-Emma
Hartford, CT
Account executive
Lawrin Rosen
Selling price
$17,000
Client
Tunxis Mgt.

A shining example among sign programs, this system comprises two directories and several "95" plaques throughout the building. It features solid brass, aluminum and stainless-steel letters, as well as aluminum name plaques mounted on slate and custom wood and PVC columns.

Fabricator
    Natural Graphics, Inc.
    Houston, TX
Designer
    Andrea Knipfel
    Natural Graphics, Inc.
Account executive
    Sharon Jackson
Client
    Windsor Residential/
    Bishop's Gate
Selling price
    $46,000

This sign package was designed to evoke the feel of an English garden, while also communicating a close-knit village atmosphere, as suggested by the brownstone-style architecture. The identity signs — which measure approximately 4 ft. 9 in. × 4 ft. 9 in.   are honed English slate, etched and paint infilled. In addition, the signs are surrounded by wrought-iron frames. In fact, these wrought-iron details are repeated on the perimeter fencing and the front door to the clubhouse/office. The secondary sign package is similar to this main identity system, using the same etched and infilled English slate and wrought-iron details.

Fabricator
True Identity
Denver, CO
Designers
Dan King
Mark Oatis
True Identity

This sign system was created for the Sunset Station Hotel and Casino. The main sign measures 47 in. wide × 52 in. high and incorporates hand-carved SignFoam® for the main copy on varigated leaf field; Gerber-router incised secondary copy with varigated leaf finish; "wax" fruit and vegetables; and a faux-grained "cabinet."

Other signs in the system include: a sandblasted redwood sign with hand-painted pictorial for the Capri Lounge; a crackle field sign for the Pizza Main Room that features a gilt border, solid timber pole with faux-rusted metal bracket and uplight sconces; a menuboard made from MDF panels with maple veneers and gilt borders, faux-rusted bracket spacers, and vinyl on magnetic sheeting; and eight 11 × 16-in. sub/ support signs with painted borders and vinyl copy.

Fabricator
Motivational Systems Inc.
National City, CA
Designer
Joy Shows
Motivational Systems

Designed for a new home community in San Diego, this system uses the shape of the logo for the sign faces, which range in size from 5 ft. × 30 in. to 15 × 16-in. wall-mounted identifications. The signs, fabricated from aluminum sheets, incorporate screen-printed graphics. The copy is created with ¼-in. painted acrylic cutouts mounted over Calon II vinyl drop shadows.

Fabricators

Potter Ornamental Iron
Dallas, TX

RBD Marble & Granite
Richardson, TX

Custom Cut Stone
Dallas, TX

Designer

Madden Marketing and Design Group
Dallas, TX

This $60,000 sign system features an 8 × 9-ft. entrance sign made from custom-cut limestone. For the "Villa Del Norte" sign, copper letters were pin-raised on the slate face; the slate was also sandblasted with an oval as background for letters, and the slate was glazed in certain areas for contrast. Interior signs incorporate Indian multicolor slate for door plaques (sandblasted and painted), as well as acrylic screened plaques inset into beveled and shaped urethane sign frames with wood posts.

Fabricator
    RB Industries
    Santee, CA
Designer
    Wieber Nelson Design
    San Diego, CA

Mira Costa College's new sign system incorporates aluminum panels with steel posts. Special fabrication techniques employed in the $150,000 system include three-color screen-printed patterns on clear, receptive vinyl wrapping posts. All sign surfaces are graffiti-coated, and the pattern is an adaptation of basket patterns from the American Indians who previously inhabited the land. The freestanding signs measure 4 × 9-ft.

Fabricator
ARTeffects, Inc.
Bloomfield, CT
Designers
New England Design
Mansfield, CT
phone

Lawrin Rosen
Harold Wood
ARTeffects, Inc.

Signs in this system have individual 8-in. brass letters with black-sprayed acrylic contours. The oval restroom signs feature cut, polished/ brushed brass and black plastic copy.

Designer
Don Bell Industries
Port Orange, FL
Designer
Walt Disney Imagineering
Celebration, FL

Don Bell Industries fabricated this wayfinding system for the Typhoon Lagoon at Walt Disney World in Orlando, FL. Most of the signs are fabricated from wood and are hand-carved to give a slightly older, distressed look. The main structure is 24 ft. high × 26 ft. wide and resembles an old pirate ship. The welcome panel is stretched canvas with painted copy. The Shark Reef sign, pictured here, measures 18 × 9 ft. and employs fiberglass for the teeth and wood for the sandblasted, hand-painted sign.

Fabricators
MCS Design & Production
Ashland, VA

Debbie D. Wallace
Richmond, VA

Designers
Al Jessee
MCS Design & Production

Debbie D. Wallace

Client
Trigon

Selling price
$5,500

The gold-medal winner in our entry monuments category is this 16-ft.-tall Olympic creation. Blurring the boundary between sign and sculpture, this structure features resculptured mannequins with togas made from muslin soaked in glue. Sandblasted, faux-finished EPS foam rocks and cut-out EPS foam capitals are also used.

Fabricator
  John Hoover
  Englewood, CO
Designers
  Andrew Trunfio
  Gary Powell
Account executive
  John Curtis
  Boyd Design Group
Client
  Rams Horn Resort
Selling price
  $10,000

The Loveland buff stone used in this sign's background was quarried in Colorado, cut into mountain shapes and inset into a dry stack wall. "Village Resort" is sandblasted and paint-filled, while the "Rams Horn" letters are brass anodized aluminum. High-density foam with a bronze faux finish is used for the ram's head.

Fabricator
  ARTeffects, Inc.
  Bloomfield, CT
Designer
  Sonalysts Studios
  Waterford, CT
Client
  Mohegan Sun Resort

This brightly colored sign features hand-pounded, ¼-in. aluminum, stud-mounted letters, as well as the Mohegan Sun Resort logo.

Fabricators
Woodgraphics
Douglasville, GA

Peachtree City Foam Craft
Tyrone, GA
Designer
Woodgraphics
Account executive
Allen DeNyse

Measuring 8 ft. 4 in. × 10 ft. 3 in., this synthetic stucco monument incorporates blue pearl marble; a black, PVC, airbrushed wood design; and "Woodgraphics" letters, a paint brush and a chisel, all hand-carved from Sign Foam® high-density urethane. The "Woodgraphics" letters use yellow and 24K goldleaf, the tip of the paint brush has 24K goldleaf, and the tip of chisel uses white goldleaf. "Sign Crafters" and "Since 1983" are made of white high-performance vinyl.

Fabricator
Natural Graphics, Inc.
Houston, TX
Designer
Susan Sharp
Natural Graphics, Inc.
Account executive
Sharon Jackson
Client
JPI/Jefferson Forest
Selling price
$13,000

This double-faced, etched and V-carved sign is inset into a structure made of the same stucco and rock used for the apartment buildings. Measuring 15 ft. 6 in. × 9 ft. 6 in., the sign includes incised copy with a rich gold infill. Also, the sign features a leaf logo that's incorporated in the wrought-iron accents.

Fabricators
Chalmers Concepts
Atlanta, GA

Mike Nicholas
Hardscapes (masonry)
Cumming, GA

Designer
Ben Robinson
Madden Marketing & Design Group
Dallas, TX

Client
Lane Co./Wellington Point
Apartment Homes

Selling price
$22,000

You can't see the Wellington Point Apartment Homes from the street; thus, this entry statement is crucial for property identification. Property brick, charcoal split-face block, cast stone and two types of granite are used within this masonry monument. The charcoal block was selected to transition the cement-colored Keystone® wall into the property.

The 8-ft.-high, 24-ft.-wide entry sign features: two detached columns; a black granite plaque inset into the brick; and a red granite insert, routed and sandblasted with logo motif. The motif piece is attached to the black main panel and projects from the surface. Gold lithochrome paint is applied in both blasted graphic areas.

Fabricators
John and Karen Ritchey
Pueblo, CO

Ken Holcombs
Range Masonry (installer)
Colorado Springs, CO

Designers
Praco Adv.
Colorado Springs, CO

Michael Brennan
Vintage Cos.
Colorado Springs, CO

Client
Charter Greens (Vintage Cos.)

Selling price
$5,800 (installation not included)

With an installed size of 3 × 18 ft., this sign has sculpted and glazed tile units, each measuring 1 sq. ft. It also features 3 in. of carved and raised bas relief with a bed depth of 1 ft. The tiles started as green (unfired) brick clay units, stacked on a slanting easel. After carving, they were colored, then taken down for drying and firing to 2300°F.

Fabricators
Woodgraphics
Douglasville, GA

Peachtree Foamcraft
Tyrone, GA

Designer
Woodgraphics

This synthetic stucco monument sign is supported by a base and columns of cultured rock. The sign background consists of dark green marble tile squares. The lettering and drop shadows consist of ⅜-in. Sintra™, with a satin gold anodized aluminum overlay. The logo panel consists of sand-blasted Sign Foam®, a Black Beauty background and a hand-carved prismatic logo with 23K gold leaf finish.

Fabricators
Woodgraphics
Douglasville, GA

Peachtree Foamcraft
Tyrone, GA

Designer
Woodgraphics

Mounted on a synthetic stucco monument, this single-faced sign consists of prismatic routed Sign Foam® with 23K gold leaf lettering and a hand-painted logo.

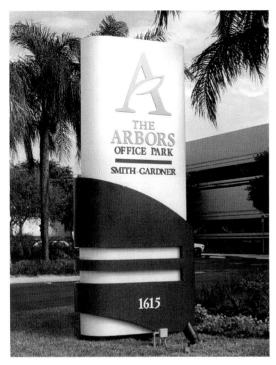

Fabricators
Woodgraphics
Douglasville, GA

Hardscapes, Inc.
Cumming, GA

Peachtree Foamcraft
Tyrone, GA
Designer
Woodgraphics
Douglasville, GA

This monument sign consists of synthetic stucco, with a centurion stone veneer applied to the columns and the lower concrete block planter. The sign background consists of cambria black granite tile with graphics and copy sandblasted and painted with Matthews gold and white enamel.

Fabricator
Don Bell Industries
Port Orange, FL
Designer
Graphics Management Group
Tampa, FL

This freestanding, double-faced, 6 × 14-ft. pylon-style sign is composed of aluminum painted with Dupont Centari™ auto enamel. A raised, decorative aluminum shroud encircles the lower portion of the oval-shaped sign. All copy and the address numerals are cut from flat, ¼-in. aluminum.

Fabricator
Sign Experts
Santa Ana, CA
Designers
Matt Triggs
GT Bicycles
Santa Ana, CA

Dave Harris
Sign Experts

This 3 × 6-ft. concrete monument incorporates a recessed graphic and dimensional, stud-mounted, aluminum, powder-coated letters.

Fabricators
Potter Ornamental Iron
Dallas, TX

RBD Marble & Granite
Richardson, TX
Designer
Madden Marketing &
Design Group
Dallas, TX

This 13-ft.-wide monument sign and planter consists of cast stone and stucco. The sign face is composed of black galaxy granite with sandblasted and painted copy/graphic.

Fabricator
  Graphic Services
  Manassas, VA
Designer
  Gary Godby
  Graphic Services
Client
  Renaissance Homes/McLean Falls
Selling price
  $3,140

You can't help but fall in love with this temporary site sign. It comprises a 4 ft. × 7 ft. 6 in. piece of MDO and an applied MDO panel with an EDGE-printed graphic. Pressure-treated 6 × 6's with MDO bases and tops are used for the sign's fluted posts. The cutouts on top are also MDO material.

Fabricator
Smith, Nelson & Oatis
Denver, CO
Designer
Mark Oatis
Smith, Nelson & Oatis
Client
Keystone Real Estate Devts.

At its highest point, this 60-ft.-long sign stands 14 ft. tall. It is made of MDF board and features hand-painted murals, clear coated to withstand the elements at 10,000 ft. above sea level.

Fabricator
Paul Fulks
Metro Sign
Arlington, TX

Designer
Ben Robinson
Madden Marketing & Design Group
Dallas, TX

Client
Intercity Investments/Villa del Norte

Selling price
$4,500

Used as a teaser announcement for a luxury apartment community under construction, this sign successfully established a waiting list of more than 200 within its first month of installation. The V-shaped Lustre Board® sign faces each measure 5 ft. × 10 ft., and are raised off the ground 3 ft. In addition, the sign comprises 4 × 4-in. pine posts covered with PVC pipes, Sign Foam® arches and molding, and a Dantex® coating. The top medallion is a resin form material, painted and applied to the surface.

Fabricator
Graphic Services
Manassas, MA
Designer
Gary Godby
Graphic Services
Client
Greenvest, L.C./Hampshire Greens

With its MDO raised border and Sintra® raised logo, letters and lines, this 6-ft. × 8-ft. 2-in. MDO sign is certainly up to par. It not only features an EDGE-printed golfer graphic, but 8 × 8-in. cedar posts whose MDO and cedar tops are stained with semi-transparent ebony stain.

Fabricator
Graphic Services, Inc.
Manassas, VA
Designer
Graphic Services, Inc.

This 4 × 8-ft. MDO sign with stock wooden columns incorporates "edge print" logos with vinyl lettering and 1-Shot Gold-painted accents.

Fabricator
Sign Concepts
Addison, IL
Designers
Al and Lynda Bolek
Sign Concepts

The lettering on this 5 × 8-ft. MDO sign is roller-blended with a stippled background.

Fabricator
Motivational Systems Inc.
National City, CA
Designer
Marjorie Wakefield
Motivational Systems Inc.

This whimsical 4 × 2-ft. sales information sign consists of a circular, painted aluminum backing with bent aluminum tubing to accentuate the sun graphic, which is composed of ½ in. acrylic pieces that are painted and glued to the backing. The copy consists of Calon II vinyl.

Fabricator
Sign Concepts
Addison, IL
Designer
Al Bolek
Sign Concepts
Client
Portillo's/Downtown Chicago

You'll lick your lips at the site of this 8 × 32-ft. painted MDO sign. This sign, as well as a similar 8 × 20-ft. sign, indicated various phases of the Portillo's construction project.

Fabricator
   Blair Sign Programs
   Alameda, CA
Designer
   Pavel Soltys
   Blair Sign Programs

These signs were fabricated for the Hamilton Air Force Base, which is the first military installation in California to be converted to private use. The large sign is a 12 × 24-ft. flexible-face type incorporating graphics created with Corel 6™, Photo Paint 6™ and Photo Touch™. The 12 × 8-ft. side signs incorporate 4-ft.-wide ovals raised 2 in. off the background. The oval graphic is flexible-face material glued to MDO with 3M™ vinyl copy on the main panels.

Fabricator
Sign Design
Wooster, OH
Designer
Ken and Stephanie Stiffler
Sign Design

This 4 × 6-ft. double-faced MDO sign incorporates vinyl lettering and graphics. The background and panels are painted with 1-Shot lettering enamel.

Fabricator
Miller Signs
Glen Rock, NJ
Designer
Will Miller
Miller Signs

This 3 × 4-ft., double-faced, hanging, post sign consists of a ¾-in.-thick MDO panel with Sign Foam® dimensional ovals (also ¾-in.-thick). The name and graphics are gilded with 23K gold and palladium leaf. Informational copy is high-performance vinyl.

Fabricator
Plamarc
São Paulo, SP
Brazil

Client
Editora Abril Jovem

Super-heroes, in natural size, guard the doors of the elevators in this publishing house of children and young adult's magazines. Each floor features one comic book hero. The panels are 0.8 x 2.1 m and were printed as one whole piece, in an electrostatic 3M™ Scotchprint. The images were transfered to an opaque vinyl with a gloss finish and then applied over the elevators' doors.

Installation and Maintenance
Publitas
São Paulo, SP
Brazil

This 60-square-meter, full-color LED, is installed in a high traffic area at Paulista Avenue, the financial heart of São Paulo. Around 85,000 vehicles use this corridor every day. The first full-color LED installed in Brazil dates from March, 1995; a full year before a similar panel made its debut in Times Square, New York.

Fabricator
Flash Neon Signs
Florianópolis, SC
Brazil

Client
Restaurant Toca da Garoupa

The fish (garoupa), lit in its submarine cave, is a single-piece sign made with metallic letters and neon, and complemented by a backlit panel. The letters at the top are lit indirectly by neon. The whole sign is 2 x 1,5 m and decorates the entrance of the restaurant in Florinópolis, SC.

Photo credit: Courtesy of Flash Neon Signs

Fabricator
Paper Express
São Paulo, SP
Brazil

Client
Museum Casa das Rosas

The flexible banners in front of the
Museum Casa das Rosas (House of Roses),
in São Paulo, give a preview of the art to
be seen inside. Both banners measure
5.1 x 1.3 m and use vinyl canvas Night &
Day by Alpargatas. The images were printed
by Xerox electrostatic 8954 and transfered
to the substrate using Fluorex paper by
Rexam. The lamination was done in a Seal
6000 and the whole project was done in
one day.

Photo credit: Homero Sérgio

Fabricator
Bureau Digital Bandeirante
São Paulo, SP
Brazil

Designer
Daniela Thomas
Standard Rio, Advertising Agency

Client
Souza Cruz

This gigantic panel, covering the south entrance of the well-known Rebouças tunnel in Rio de Janeiro is 13 m high and 90 m wide. The piece was printed directly over a vinyl banner material by Sansuy, using the large format printers, Vutek's 1660 and 3200i. Positioned in a high traffic place, the banner advertises a Jazz Festival, sponsored by the cigarette company Souza Cruz.

Part of the same campaign, eight balls, with four different designs, floated in the Rodrigo de Freitas Lagoon, in Rio de Janeiro. Printed on both sides of a vinyl material using the Vutek 3200i, the balls were lit from the inside at night to glow over the lagoon with its message. Their diameters measured 5 to 7 m.

Fabricator
All Signs
São Paulo, SP
Brazil

Client
Vício

This panel was printed directly over a piece of brushed aluminum by a large format digital printer — Michelangelo, from LAC of Japan. The panel sets the tone of the window setting at the fashion store Vício, at one of the most recognizable malls in São Paulo City.

Photo credit: Courtesy of Antônio Peticov

Fabricator
Antônio Peticov
São Paulo, SP
Brazil

Designer
Antônio Peticov
São Paulo, SP
Brazil

Client
Companhia do Metropolitano de São Paulo (Metrô)

São Paulo City's subway system decided to bring a bit of art to the life of the 2.5 million people that use its trains ever yday. For the Praça da República Station, Antônio Peticov created an installation using hand-painted ceramic tiles, backlit and stainless steel, to honor the Brazilian writer Oswald de Andrade and the Modern Cultural Movement of the 1930s. The ceiling was backlit, painted with a stretched image of Oswald de Andrade. The same image is reflected by a stainless steel pole, 30 cm in diameter, without any distortion. The tiles at the top and bottom of the mural reproduce parts of the work done by the modernist painter, Tarsila do Amaral. The phrase "Tupy or Not Tupy" was cast on cement. The whole mural is 16 x 3,5 m and took 8 months to be completed from conception to final installation.

Fabricator
Bureau Digital Bandeirante
São Paulo, SP
Brazil

Client
Antarctica

The flexible side of this truck uses a vinyl material by Sansuy, that made this digital work possible. The whole piece was printed in a large format inkjet printer by Vutek and then fashioned as a curtain to the side of the truck.

Acolite Claud United, 54
Ad-Art Electronic Sign Corp., 57
All Signs, 183
Alvey's Signs, Inc., 58
Arrow Sign Co., 13, 35, 41, 81
Art Frisbie's Airworx, 95
Artcraft Signs & Graphics, 97
ARTeffects, Inc., 25, 32, 33, 42, 43, 47, 50, 58, 59, 62, 107,
    117, 140, 156, 163, 165
Auto Graphix, 138

Bentsen Signs, 105, 113
Bert Graphix, 132, 133, 134, 135, 136, 137, 138, 139
Blair Sign Programs, 176
Boyd Design Group, 104
Bureau Digital Bandeirante, 182, 184

California Neon Products, 48, 60
California Signs & Designs, 123, 149
Capital Neon, 82, 83
Carlson Sign Art, 103, 112, 118
Chalmers Concepts, 167
Cinnabar, 60
Classic Design Studio, 96, 111, 120, 122, 146, 147, 149
Cleveland Metroparks, 152
Colorburst Signs and Graphics, 143
Commercial Neon Signs, 16
Creative Neon Works, Inc., 8, 37
Custom Art & Signs, 89
Custom Craftsman Signs, 110
Custom Cut Stone, 161
Custom Neon Designs, Inc., 76
Custom Signs, 90

D&D Signs, 91
DH Signs of the Times, 103
David Design, 86, 111
Display Ad Intl., 60
Display Solutions SA (PTY) Ltd., 56
Don Bell Industries, 163, 169

Endless Possibilities, 102
Enseicom Signs, Inc., 15
Eric Grohe Design, 126, 127, 128, 129, 130, 131

Festival Sign Service, 123
Figula Designs, 67
Figula Neon, 67
Flash Neon Signs, 180
Fluoresco, 77

Goodnough, Mark, 119
Gordon Sign Co., 33, 34, 35, 36, 81
Grand Illusions, Inc., 148
Graphic Services, 170, 173, 174
Graphic Systems Inc., 54
Great Big Signs, Inc., 116
Gulf State Plastics, Inc., 26

Hardscapes, Inc.,167, 169
Hoboken Sign, Co., 19
Hoover, John, 165
Hunter's Mfg., Inc., 17, 20, 68

Image Works, Inc., 12, 29
Imaginality, Inc., 135
Imperial Sign Corp., 10, 55
Independent Sign Co., 27, 63
Island Designs, 101, 109

Jakes Crane & Rigging, 60
Jayco Signs, Inc., 26

Karman Ltd., 151
Keene Signworx, 106, 109, 119
Kish, Chuck, 97
Kraft Studio, 72, 73
Kullman Industries, 18

LA Signs and Graphics, 148, 151
Landmark Sign Co., 65, 79
Living Color, Inc., 12

MCM Graphix, 92, 99, 124, 125, 145
MCS Design & Production, 164
Mer-Vac, 70
Metro Sign, 172
Miller Signs, 177
Moran Canvas, 48
Morris Signs, 28
Morse, Mary, 106
Motivational Systems, Inc., 94, 160, 175
Munoz, Mario, 116

National Neon, 17, 20, 65, 68, 79
National Sign Corp., 6, 9, 14, 21, 22, 25, 26, 40, 42, 43,
   44, 53, 68, 74, 82
National Signs Inc, 77
Natural Graphics, Inc., 157, 166
Neon Knights, Inc., 6, 71
Neon Latitudes, 64, 70
Neon-Line Werbedesign GmbH, 7, 69, 75, 78, 79
Neon Pro Signs, 66
Neon Products, 41, 61, 69, 78
Neotericity, 72
Northport WoodSmiths, 117

Olde Lang Signs, 107
One Truck Parade, 93
Orde Adv. Inc., 11, 83

Paper Express, 181
Paris Signs, 155
Peachtree City Foam Craft, 166, 168, 169
Peticov, Antônio, 184
Plamarc, 178
Potter Ornamental Iron, 161, 169
Princeton Welding, 13
Publitas, 179

RB Industries, 162
RBD Marble & Granite, 161, 169
Range Masonry, 167
Reid Signs, 134
Ritchey, Jon and Karen, 113, 167
Ross, Greg, 88

Shaw Sign & Awning, Inc., 31
Shawcraft Sign Co., 93, 107, 125, 144
Sign Classics, 110, 119
Sign Concepts, 100, 124, 143, 144, 145, 174, 175
Sign Crafters, 28
Sign Design, 91, 99, 124, 177
Sign Experts, 169
Sign It, 92, 104, 105, 112, 118
Sign Productions, Inc., 30, 59, 83
Signature Signs, Inc., 61
Signcraft, 102
Signs, Inc, 145
Signworks, 129
Simington Electrical Adv., 10
Smith, Nelson & Oatis, 171
Solar Graphics, Inc., 121, 122
Sunbelt Metals and Mfg., Inc., 148
Superior Sign Systems, 49, 74, 80

T&L Displays, 24
Tobey Archer Studio, 70
Tower Structures, 10
Tramps Designs, 141, 142, 143
True Identity, 98, 108, 114, 115, 116, 129, 150, 158
Tullochgorum Signs, 87, 96

US Signs, 108
USA Signs of America, Inc., 18
Ultraneon Sign Co., 7, 38, 39, 46
Union Structural Eng., 56
United Structural Eng., 56

Vegas Steel, 60
Vinyl Signs, 100
Vital Signs, 98, 101

Wallace, Debbie D., 164
Walton Signage, 80
Western Signs, 154
White Way Sign, 52
Woodgraphics, 166, 168, 169

Young Electric Sign Co., 17, 23

Ad-Art Electronic Sign Corp., 57
Alpine Signs, 95
Amenta-Emma, 156
Antista Design, 80
Arrow Sign Co., 35, 41, 81
Art Frisbee's Airworx, 95
Artcraft Signs & Graphics, 97
ARTeffects, 25, 32, 33, 43, 47, 50, 58, 59, 62, 107, 140, 163
Aslami, Sayed, 49
Auto Graphix, 138

Bender Wells Clark Design, 28
Bentsen Signs, 105, 113
Bert Graphix, 132, 133, 134, 135, 136, 137, 138, 139
Bishop Museum, 145
Blair Sign Programs, 176
Bloomington Design, 111
Boyd Design Group, 104
Butler, David, 115, 116

California Neon Products, 60
California Signs & Designs, 123, 149
Canadian Museum of Civilizations, 66
Capital Neon, 82, 83
Carlson Sign Art, 112, 118
Classic Design Studio, 96, 111, 120, 122, 146, 147
Cleveland Metroparks, 152
Creative Neon Works, Inc., 8, 37
Custom Art & Signs, 89
Custom Craftsman Signs, 110
Custom Signs, 90

D&D Signs, 91
DH Sign of the Times, 103
Dailey & Assoc. Adv., 60
David Design, 86, 111
Debra Nichols Design, 74
Design Partnership, 44
Design Works, 10
Dunlavey, Michael, 154

Endless Possibilities, 102
Eric Grohe Design, 126, 127, 128, 129, 130, 131

Festival Sign Service, 123
Figula Designs, 67
Figula Neon, 67
Fluoresco, 77
Freedman Tung & Bottomley, 13
Fulkerson, Annie, 64

GT Bicycles, 169
Gahwiler & Assoc., 56
Gordon Sign Co., 35, 36
Gotham City, 16
Graphic Management Group, 169
Graphic Services, 170, 173, 174
Graphic Solutions, 17, 23, 39
Grand Illusions, Inc., 148
Great Big Signs, Inc., 116

Hammond, Marty, 143
Hessler, Susan, 155
Hoboken Sign Co., 19
Hueg, Bill, 114
Hunter's Mfg., Inc., 17

Illume Creatif, 76
Image Works, Inc, 12, 29
Imaginality, Inc., 135
Interarc., 81
Island Designs, 101, 109

J. Newbold Assoc., 48
J.H. Bradburn & Assoc., PC, 34
Johnson Design Group, 103

K&Co., 24
Keene Signworx, 109, 119
Kelman, Uri, 108
Kish, Chuck, 97
Kraft Studio, 72, 73
Kramer, Maria-Rosa, 75
Kraus, Arch Johannes, 75
Kullman Industries, 18

LA Signs and Graphics, 148, 151
Lance Jackson & Assoc., 33
Landmark Sign Co., 17, 20, 65, 68, 79
Living Color, Inc., 12
Lopez-Bonilla, Juan, 58

MCM Graphix, 92, 99, 124, 125, 145
MCS Design & Production, 164
Madden Marketing and Design Group, 161, 167, 169, 172
Mendoza, John, 113
Miller Signs, 177
Motivational Systems, Inc., 94, 160, 175

National Sign Corp., 6, 9, 14, 21, 22, 25, 26, 40, 42, 43, 68, 74, 82
National Signs Inc., 77
Natural Graphics, Inc., 157, 166
Neon Knights, Inc., 6, 71
Neon Latitudes, 64, 70
Neon-Line Werbedesign GmbH, 7, 69, 75, 78, 79
Neon Pro Signs, 66
Neon Products, 41, 61, 69, 78
Neotericity, 72
New England Design, 25, 47, 50, 163
Niemitz Design Group, 43
Noel Davies & Assoc., 10
Nolin Larosee Design Communications, 15
Northport WoodSmiths, 117

Olde Boise Guitar Co., 146
One Truck Parade, 93
Orde Adv. Inc., 11, 83

Panda Mgt., 38
Peticov, Antônio, 184
Plancom Design Team, 52
Powell, Gary, 165
Praco Adv., 167

Rainwater Design, 43
Raven Interior Design, Inc, 55
Reid Signs, 134
Ritchey, Jon, 113
Ross, Greg, 88

Shaw Sign & Awning, Inc., 31
Shawcraft Sign Co., 93, 107, 125, 144
Sign Classics, 110, 119
Sign Concepts, 100, 124, 143, 144, 145, 174, 175
Sign Crafters, 28
Sign Design, 91, 99, 124, 177
Sign Experts, 169
Sign It, 92, 104, 105, 112, 118
Sign Productions, Inc., 30
Signature Signs, Inc., 61
Signcraft, 102
Signworks, 129
Simington Electrical Adv., 10
Smith, Nelson & Oatis, 27, 63, 171
Solar Graphics, Inc., 121, 122
Sonalyst Studios, 42, 117, 165
Stancel, Doug, 59, 83
Stewart, Dan, 58
Superior Sign Systems, 80

TRA Graphic Design, 53
Thomas, Daniela, 182
Tobey Archer Studio, 70
Tom Graboski Assoc., Inc., 54
Tramps Designs, 141, 142, 143, 143
True Identity, 98, 108, 114, 115, 116, 129, 150, 158
Truntio, Andrew, 165
Tullochgorum Signs, 87, 96

Ultraneon Sign Co., 7, 38, 46

Vintage Cos., 167
Vital Signs, 98, 100, 101

WDIFL Creative, 148
Walsh & Assoc., 25
Walt Disney Imagineering, 163
Walton Signage, 80
Wieber Nelson Design, 151, 162
Weil, Ron, 64
Woodgraphics, 166, 168, 169

Yasvin Design, 119

Sign design and fabrication books available from ST Publications

Carving Signs
Commercial Sign Techniques: Step-by-Step
Complete Guide to Truck Lettering, Pinstriping and Graphics
Engineering Sign Structures: An Introduction to Analysis and Design
Gold Leaf Techniques 4th Edition
Gráficos de Vinilo
In-Store Signage & Graphics: Connecting with Your Customer
Light Artist Anthology: Neon and related media
Mastering Layout
Neon World
Neon Techniques 4th Edition
Neon: The Next Generation
New Let There Be Neon
Sign Design and Layout
Sign Design Gallery 2
Sign Gallery
Sign Structures and Foundations
Sign User's Guide: A Marketing Aid
Vinyl Graphics How-to: Master Principles
Vinyl Graphics & Auto Decor Video Instruction Series

For a complete catalog of books and trade magazines, contact:

ST Publications, Inc.
407 Gilbert Avenue
Cincinnati, Ohio 45202
U.S.A.
Tel. 513-421-2050
Fax 513-421-6110
Website: www.stpubs.com